Sail The Dream

Beginner Cruising - Everything needs to Know (Paperwork, money and time-saving, location, booking, and packing) this Complete travel guide help to make your cruise plan.

Carlton Napper

COPYRIGHT © 2022 by Carlton Napper

No part of this book may be stored in any retrieval system, photocopied, recorded, scanned, or transmitted in any form, or reproduced in any form, without the written permission of the author

Legal & Disclaimer

The content and information in this book have been provided for educational and entertainment purposes only. While every effort has been made to confirm the information provided in this eBook, neither the author nor the distributor accepts responsibility for any errors or omissions.

This book's materials should not be construed as personal medical advice or instruction. so, The information contained in this book and its contents is not designed to replace or take the place of any form of medical or professional advice; and is not meant to replace the need for independent medical, financial, legal, or other professional advice or services, as may be required.

The facts and opinions presented here are thought to be factual and sound, based on the best judgment available to the readers. The content and information contained in this book have been compiled from sources deemed reliable, and it is accurate to the best of the Author's knowledge, information, and belief.

Where appropriate and/or necessary, readers should seek the advice of a qualified professional (including but not limited to your doctor, attorney, financial advisor, or such other professional advisor).

DEDICATION

This book is dedicated to my excellent readers
To those who are unwittingly lucky

Table Of Content

INTRODUCTION 15

Chapter -1 16

  What are you going on a cruise for? 16

    The Tale : 16

      Modern equipment aboard cruise ships 16

      The motivations for a cruise: 17

      Cruise on Value: 17

      Cruise On Romance: 17

      Take A Kitchen Cruise: 17

      Take A Diversity Cruise: 18

      Take An ACTIVITY Cruise: 18

      Take A Cruise For Simplicity: 18

      Take A Family Cruise: 18

      Take A Satisfaction Cruise: 18

Chapter -2 19

  What is a cruise line? 19

    List of the most popular cruise lines: 19

    Birka line: 19

    Carnival cruise lines: 20

    Crystal cruise lines: 20

    Disney cruise lines: 20

    Norwegian cruise lines: 21

Chapter -3 22

  Cruise Patrol: Find the greatest discounts on various cruises 22

    The greatest techniques to arrange your finest cruises 24

    Cruise Critic - Your one-stop shop for cruise information 27

Current forecasts of cruise ship reviews 30

Find the greatest cruise deals 31

Chapter -4 33

Choose the cruise lines that are perfect for you 33

Cruise comments: what to anticipate from a cruise 35

What to look for on a cruise 37

The past, present, and future voyage 39

History and development 40

Cruises now 41

Cruise of the future 42

What else can you anticipate from these cruises? 42

1. Holland America Noordam Cruise Ship: 42

2. NCL America's Pride of Hawaii: 43

3. Royal Caribbean Freedom of the Seas: 43

4. The Crown Princess of New Princess Cruises: 43

5. The new cruise line, Princess Cruises 44

6. MSC Musica: 44

7. CostaConcordia by Costa Cruises: 44

Chapter -5 46

What are some of the greatest closed-loop cruise itineraries? 46

Fort Lauderdale to Bahamas, Mexico, and Grand Cayman: 46

Los Angeles to the Mexican Riviera : 47

Seattle to Alaska, the Inside Passage, and Dawes Glacier: 47

Fort Lauderdale to Puerto Rico, St. Thomas, and St. Kitts: 48

Fort Lauderdale to Key West, Belize, and Grand Cayman: 49

Cape Liberty to Bermuda: 50

Chapter -6 51

16 Cruise Tips for First-Timers 51

Chapter :7 57

When Is the Most Appropriate Time to Book a Cruise? 57

- How far ahead of time should you plan a cruise? 57
- What are the advantages of booking a cruise in advance? 58
- Best Options for Lodging 58
- Main Dining Room Preferred Times 59
- Make a reservation for popular shore excursions and onboard activities. 59
- Cancellation Policy for Early Bookings 59

Chapter -8 60

When Is the Best Time to Travel by Cruise Ship? 60

- Alaska: 60
- Caribbean: 60
- Mediterranean: 61
- Northern Europe: 62
- Asia: 63
- South America and Antarctica: 63
- Galapagos: 64
- Hawaii: 64

Chapter-9 66

What are the advantages of last-minute cruise bookings? 66

- How can I obtain a huge discount on last-minute cruises? 66
- A fantastic cruise deal is available at the last minute 68
- What's the best way to find the best cruise deals? 70
- How can I obtain the finest last-minute cruise deals? 70
- When is the best month to go on a cruise? 71
- Cruises on the cheap are a fantastic way to spend your holiday. 71
- What else is included in the Economy Cruise package? 72
- What will you encounter on your journey? 72

Do cruises get less costly as the departure date approaches?.............74

Find the greatest bargain on last-minute cruises. 75

Basic strategies and tips for securing a last-minute cruise: 76

Some pointers to help you discover the greatest last-minute cruise :..77

CHAPTER -10 78

While you're on a cruise, book a cruise. 78

When is the best time to schedule an Alaska cruise? 79

When is the best time to plan a Caribbean cruise?................................79

Chapter -11 80

Taking Care of a Fantastic Opportunity on a Cruise Ship 80

Some things to consider before applying for a cruise ship job: 81

Relax and enjoy your cruise holiday. 82

The measures to follow to guarantee a pleasant cruise: 83

To minimize annoyance, plan your cruise holiday ahead of time 85

The fundamentals of economic cruises are discussed 87

How to acquire a cruise at a lower price 89

You intend to go on a cruise that is within your budget. What's the best way to obtain one? 90

So, when you're ready, here are some recommendations to help you save money on your luxury cruise: 91

Cheap cruises provide a fantastic holiday at a minimal cost.................92

Here are some pointers to keep in mind if you wish to go on a cruise on a budget:...93

The top cruises have been chosen 94

Singles Cruises: The Best Place for Singles to Meet Other Singles 97

Here are some thorough guidelines to assist you in making your decision:..98

Chapter -12 99

The Best Ways to Get Ready for Your First Cruise.................................99

Chapter -13 104

The Only Cruise Packing List You'll Ever Need 104

What should I take on a cruise in terms of clothes, shoes, and accessories? 104

What hygiene items should I bring on a cruise? 108

What papers should I bring on a cruise? 109

Wallet and Money Belt Accessories 109

Contact Information & Documentation 109

What technological things should I bring on a cruise? 110

What else should I bring on a cruise? 110

Checklist for Packing for a Cruise 111

Chapter -14 116

Add These 13 Eco-Friendly Shore Excursions to Your Bucket List 116

Chapter -15 120

Take a break and enjoy Alaska Cruise's thrills and excitement 120

The fundamentals of an Alaska cruise 122

With Caribbean cruises, you may discover the magnificence 123

Carnival Cruises - Take a cruise trip with one of the world's most well-known cruise lines 126

Obtain the services of a cruise professional 127

Carnival Cruise Lines offers a luxurious way to travel. 128

On a Carnival Fun Ship, you may enjoy the following activities and amenities: 130

Celebrity Cruises provides you with friendly and attentive service ... 131

Celebrity Cruise Line offers an all-inclusive holiday 133

Disney cruises are a dream come true for many people 136

Disney Cruise Line - For the Happiness of Your Child 138

Spend Your Cruise To Your Dream Destination With Hawaii Cruises. 140

A Mediterranean cruise is a fantastic way to spend your vacation.... 142

Norwegian Cruise Lines invites you to have a cruise vacation onboard 145

Escape to paradise with Princess Cruises 147

With the Princess Cruises fleet, you may travel to more places 150

Royal Caribbean Cruises offer a luxurious way to visit the island 153

Exploring the Long Chain Islands takes a long time.............................154

Why should you book a cruise with Royal Caribbean?........................155

Chapter -16..158

How to Take a Luxury Cruise Around the World 158

North America is located in North America :...................................158

The Caribbean is a beautiful place:...158

South America is a continent in South America: 159

Galapagos blue-footed boobies:..159

Europe:..159

Asia: 159

Australia, New Zealand, and the South Pacific are all part of the South Pacific region: 160

Africa:..160

Antarctica:..160

Cruises around the United States:..160

Make arrangements for a luxury cruise around the world: 161

Chapter -17..162

Welcome To The Cruise 162

TURN IT ON!..166

LOCATION, LOCATION, LOCATION...169

More Than Journeys By Bus...170

FOOD, FOOD, FOOD..174

Getting Ready To Drink..178

Mama Is In Need Of A New Pair Of Shoes 181

Sports And Other Activities 181

Take Me Away, Calgon! 183

Oh My Painful Tummy 184

NO MONEY!, NO MONEY!, NO MONEY! 185

GENERALLY 186

Chapter-18 188

How to Avoid Getting Seasick on a Cruise 188

What causes motion sickness at sea? 188

On a cruise, how long does seasickness last? 188

Which cruise ships are the best for avoiding seasickness? 188

On a trip, where is the greatest spot to sail to prevent becoming seasick? 189

On a cruise, where is the ideal cabin to prevent motion sickness? 190

What are the options for treating seasickness on a cruise? 191

Acupuncture and acupressure: 191

a breath of fresh air: 191

What should I eat and drink on a cruise ship to prevent motion sickness? 192

Chapter-19 193

The Ultimate Guide to Cruising with a Toddler 193

When should a youngster be old enough to go on a cruise? 193

Which cruises are the greatest for toddlers? 193

Cruises departing from ports near your home city : 194

Cruises with a shorter duration: 194

Cruises to places that are suitable for families: 194

Are cruises enjoyable for toddlers? 194

What should I bring on a cruise with my toddler? 195

Which stateroom is ideal for families sailing with a toddler? 196

On a cruise, are there any babysitter services available for toddlers? 197

On a cruise, what will my kid eat? 198

Is it necessary for me to carry a stroller? 198

What kinds of beach excursions am I allowed to do with my toddler? 198

Chapter-20 200

What is Accessible Travel for Seniors with Disabilities? 200

Information to Bring With You Checklist 202

Your Legal Rights: 203

Accessible Cruising is a great way to get there 204

Wheelchair-Friendly Travel Resources 204

Autism and Traveling 205

More Apps and Online Resources 206

Everything You Need to Know About Cruises for Seniors with Disabilities 207

Chapter-21 211

Everything You Need to Know About Getting Married at Sea 211

Is getting married on a cruise ship legal? 211

Is it legal to marry aboard a ship in international waters? 211

What is the cost of getting married on a cruise ship? 212

Is it possible to marry a ship's captain at sea? 212

On a ship, how do you organize a wedding? 213

Are our wedding planners available on cruise ships? 213

What is the greatest cruise ship for a wedding? 213

Is it possible to have a same-sex marriage at sea? 214

What should I do if I want to propose on a cruise? 214

Chapter-22 216

The Ultimate Honeymoon Cruise Planning Guide 216

Chapter-23 221

From Florida, these are the top five Thanksgiving cruises. 221

From Tampa, go to the Caribbean and the Americas 221

From Fort Lauderdale, go to the Panama Canal and the Southern Caribbean 222

From Miami, go to Key West and the Bahamas 224

Chapter-24 227

9 Places to Visit on New Year's Eve in 2022 227

St. Kitts and Nevis 227

Singapore 228

Dominican Republic, Puerto Plata 228

The Galapagos Islands are a group of islands off the coast of Ecuador 229

Florida's Key West 229

Patagonia 229

The Virgin Islands, United States of America 230

Bangkok is the capital of Thailand 231

New Zealand is a country in the Pacific Ocean 231

Chapter-25 232

In 2022, there are 8 incredible places to spend Christmas on the beach 232

Nassau is the capital of the Bahamas 232

Curacao 233

Cozumel 234

Jamaica 234

St. Kitts and Nevis 235

St. Croix is a small island in the Caribbean 236

Cayman Islands 237

St. Thomas is the patron saint of sailors 238

Chapter-26 239

11 Spectacular Places to Visit on Your Birthday 239

Chapter-27 245

Everything You Need to Know About Purchasing Souvenirs in Port 245

Mother's Day Travel Gifts for Mom: 18 Ideas 248

For Father's Day, here are 14 great travel gifts for Dad 255

12 Gifts for the Cruiser in Your Life 261

Chapter-28 266

On a cruise, there are 19 things you should avoid doing 266

Chapter-29 272

Which Way Should I Wrap It Up? 272

INTRODUCTION

The lyrics of Frankie Ford's song "Sea Cruise" appear to match the thoughts of many individuals while planning to travel. Some believe it's out of the range of possibilities when planning a holiday on a budget, but not anymore!

Many people believe that traveling the wide seas aboard a luxury ship is a holiday we can't possibly daydream about. However, with some proper budget planning, a cruise is well within the range of possibilities! The cost of cruising has plummeted considerably over the past several years, and it's become accessible for practically everyone as a holiday option.

But most of us might afford to cruise that much more regularly if we could only cut down on all the additional onboard and on-shore charges, above and beyond the real cruise ticket. There are lots of advice on how and where to save costs on your trip. Whether you seek recommendations from family members and friends, the Internet, or your regional travel agency, they are are useful. The only thing is how do you remember them all? This book has collected the greatest suggestions from numerous sources and placed them in one easy location - HERE!

Almost anybody may have a cruise holiday that's everything shown in the movies and on television. You may visit The Bahamas, Hawaii, Mexico, and even Alaska on luxurious cruise ships with all the facilities of a resort on land.

The best way to make the most out of your cruise holiday is to realize where you may save cost without losing fun or relaxation. Many cruises are indeed, but that doesn't always imply "ALL inclusive". There are additional costs for things on board while also activities and beach visits. You deserve to enjoy your trip and everything that comes with it, and you can do it on a spending plan! What could be great than that?

So sit back and read up on the best methods to save costs on your trip. Gopher, Julie, and Doc from "The Love Boat" won't be there, but YOU will be!

Chapter -1

What are you going on a cruise for?

Do you have any notion what a cruise is?
You'd guess he was talking to Hollywood star Tom Cruise, right?

Well, you are wrong. (Is this a game show?) Seriously, cruises are getting more and more popular with individuals, families, or groups trying to unwind differently. Want to know more about cruises? Read on to discover out what it is and why you should select a cruise on your next holiday.

Cruising often refers to marine cruises lasting a few days or longer. It is carried out on boats, sailboats, and motorboats, perfect for journeys of 3 or 4 days. However, if the cruise lasts a week or more and the journey involves numerous locations on extensive itineraries, strong and massively constructed cruise lines are chosen.

The Tale :

The concept for the voyage arose after Joshua Slocum, a retired captain, traversed the globe between 1895 and 1898. Although going around the globe was just unthinkable at the time, Slocum adapted his 37ft sloop named Spray and sailed around the world on his own.

Modern equipment aboard cruise ships: From there, strategies are created that make navigating feasible and more pleasant. In addition to standard navigation and navigation skills, cruise ships utilize propulsion systems on their vessel.

Electricity is currently utilized to power cruise systems (such as lighting, communications devices, and the like) (such as lights, communications devices, and the like).

In addition to the power provided by the internal engines, there are additional generators, solar panels, and wind turbines for extra energy sources, particularly during lengthy trips. Communication on board is also becoming prevalent aboard cruise ships. In addition to the classic SSB shortwave marine radio, which incurs no operational expenses and enables e-mail to be sent and received, newer ships are now outfitted with satellite telephone systems.

The motivations for a cruise: It covers the history of the cruise ship and the potential services that you may anticipate on board. Still, searching for convincing reasons why you should take a cruise on your next vacation?

Cruise on Value: A cruise package contains practically everything you need aboard. The cabin you stay in, your dining requirements, onboard entertainment, and more to make you feel just at home, all for the price of one.

Cruise On Romance: If you're traveling on a cruise with your spouse or wife, enjoy quiet beaches at each stop, balcony dining with great sea views, and spa options for two. You may also have a romantic supper each evening in the main dining area.

Take A Kitchen Cruise: Prepare to gain seven pounds every week with these tasty snacks supplied aboard. Dishes are presented with a range of unusual ingredients and cooking ways. Good side meals like pizza and ice cream and spa food are also healthy options. You may also eat in a tiny bistro or a casual restaurant.

Take A Diversity Cruise: Several possibilities are accessible to you: 150 distinct ships, 1,800 marinas, and a large selection of attractions and activities. Find out the number of possibilities available to build the ideal cruise for you.

Take An ACTIVITY Cruise: Onboard, there will be activities to keep you occupied. There are tourist and sporting activities, cultural events, educational tours with chosen historians and educators, or you can simply lay by the pool and rest.
The concert continues till late at night. Enjoy the dance revolution, Broadway-style musical performances, try your luck at the gaming stations, or just spend the night on the ship's balcony admiring the magnificent sky.

Take A Cruise For Simplicity: Unlike backpackers, where you need this travel card to locate accommodations or places to eat on, aboard a cruise liner all you need is a travel agent to take care of all the logistics. When you are on board, practically all of your bills are covered, you just have to enjoy eating it.

Take A Family Cruise: It's a family vacation. Kids' food and activities will keep them occupied and happy while you give yourself some time.

Take A Satisfaction Cruise: Whatever your price, cruise companies make sure all packages have 24/7 first-call assistance. Satisfaction guaranteed. Take a cruise on your next holiday.

Chapter -2

What is a cruise line?

A firm or organization handles the cruises. Cruise companies have two aims. First for the transit industry and second for the leisure sector. In addition to administrative officers and headquarters personnel, cruise line staff, headed by the ship's captain and crew, as well as hospitality staff led by a hotel manager, are distributed throughout the voyage.

Among the cruise lines now operational, some are the direct heirs of old passenger lines. Others were among the first cruise lines launched in the early 1960s. Having a cruise business upfront is like putting your money in danger. A little decline in cruise reservations might result in the loss of your company as you will have to return all expenditures invested for the building of the cruise ship.

List of the most popular cruise lines:

There are now 52 cruise lines in the United States, Europe, Asia, and beyond. Most of these cruise lines are headquartered in the United States, the others in different European nations.

Here are some of the cruise lines:

Birka line:

An Aldan shipping firm concentrates on Baltic Sea cruise operations using Stockholm as the starting point. He was born in 1971 following the purchase of the ship M / S Princess, which would eventually become Prinsessan. He took his maiden voyage between Stockholm and Mariehamn.

In 1972, Birka Line purchased the M / S Olav and renamed it, Baroness. In prior years, they had only acquired a couple more ships. They also provide vehicle and passenger ferries on the Stockholm-Helsinki route. One of the additions is the M / S Drottningen, a rail ferry servicing the Stockholm-Helsinki / Leningrad route.

Carnival cruise lines:

It is currently a division of Carnival Corporation, which runs multiple cruise lines and has developed into the biggest firm in the cruise industry. Carnival Cruise Lines pioneered the notion of cheaper and shorter voyages. They were able to construct bigger ships, notably the Carnival Destiny, which weighs 101,000 tonnes and has become the biggest passenger ship in the world.

Currently, in the first quarter of 2006, the corporation announced the addition of two additional boats to its fleet. These are Carnival Freedom, which launched in 2007, and Carnival Splendor, which will open in spring 2008.

Crystal cruise lines:

More widely known as Crystal Cruises, Crystal Cruise Lines launched in 1988 with its three mid-size and high-end ships. It is owned by a prominent Japanese shipping corporation, Nippon Yusen Kaisha Line. Their ships are consistently ranked by Conde Nast Traveler magazine as one of the top cruise lines. Even in most travel books, all three ships are in the top 20 of all cruise ships now in operation.

Disney cruise lines:

As the name indicates, it is owned by the famed Walt Disney Company and is based in Celebration, Florida. It runs two cruise lines: Disney Magic and Disney Wonder and Castaway Cay, an island in the Bahamas built as an exclusive stopover for Disney ships.

The first ship, Disney Magic, started operating on July 30, 1998. The other, the Disney Wonder, premiered on August 15, 1999. Each of the ships has 875 staterooms and a crew of 945. Its design is generally the same, with slight differences in the dining and recreation sections. Both boats contain spaces for various age groups including toddlers, toddlers, teenagers, and adults.

Norwegian cruise lines:

The corporation is located in Miami, Florida, and was formed in 1966 as Norwegian Caribbean Lines. He began by selling Caribbean cruises at incredible pricing.

The purchase of the cruise ship France in 1979, subsequently transformed and named Norway, cleared the stage for the new era of huge cruise companies. Other cruise lines provide numerous trip packages to make your cruise holiday special.

Chapter -3

Cruise Patrol: Find the greatest discounts on various cruises

Cruises are one of the most popular holiday activities nowadays. It is a really gratifying journey since it is unlike anything you have encountered before. Cruising requires years of travel, unlike your other pastimes where you just spend 10-14 days. You would have to spend years sailing if you intend to tour the globe and see various destinations in the area. Be prepared for varied encounters when you visit other countries which may provide you with fresh things to remember.

Cruises provide another sensation of fulfillment and pleasure. It is the fastest expanding industry in the travel world. There are over 1,800 ports across the globe for you to experience the safest and most secured areas. It's not just enjoyable but fulfilling too.

It is also a strategy to make your trip a fantastic vacation. This is what a lot of folks like. However, you have to patrol to locate the greatest cruise bargain accessible. You have to locate someone who can offer you all the enjoyment you need. This comprises the whole spectrum of diverse services that a cruise ship may provide. When you patrol on a cruise ship, these are the things you need to find to enjoy your years on the ship. The boat must contain:

- a sophisticated or informal dinner

- 24-hour service

- Bowl

- entertainment centers

- entertainment centers

- Shopping centers
- Bars, discos, and clubs
- Leisure facilities
- Wellness and fitness center
- Emergency clinic
- Medical centers
- Beauty salons and day spas
- Mess
- Souvenir shop
- the spaces
- Food centers and many more

These items are your top priority on your voyage. You must locate all these amenities to enjoy your stay.

There are a few questions to clarify regarding your cruise excursion. Before organizing your vacation reservation, you should conduct a little study on what to consider. You must answer all of these questions correctly:

- Think about your reasons for deciding to go on a cruise.
- You also need to determine whether you want to enjoy cruises.
- Know the precise location of your voyage. Do you like a deep-sea cruise or something else when there are activities?
- Know your aim, whether you want to rest, relax or embark on an adventure.
- Know whether you are interested in exploring the globe.

• What locations do you wish to visit?

There are a few things to consider when picking a certain cruise. While sailing, you need to know the length or duration of your voyage.

You should also know about the numerous sorts of cruises offered. It's a terrific approach to advise you on what to choose before you buy a cruise. You need to know the sorts to determine which is the greatest form of cruise that matches your likes. Sailing is mainly about relaxing on board while having time to tour the globe. Land at various ports where you may explore diverse cultures and customs. You should always bear in mind that you will require a lot of money to go on a cruise.

You have to choose the cruise ship which offers all the amenities you need at a moderate cost. Not only do you have to look for the lowest price, but you also have to pick the one that will assure your stay on board. The introduction of special cruisers with skilled survival troops. They will safeguard and monitor all of your actions on board. You will also take care of your children's activities to maintain a safe atmosphere for them.

If you want to locate the finest rates on your trip, you may need to utilize the internet to supply you with the information you need. Some websites may provide you with the finest bargain for you to enjoy your voyage around the globe.

The greatest techniques to arrange your finest cruises

Most individuals dream about enjoying a boat holiday. It doesn't emphasize enough that you shouldn't base your cruise decision on pricing alone. You too, go on vacation to have fun and have fun.

For your cruise trip to be a success, you must have a strategy before picking a specific cruise. First, most cruises include facilities and services such as meals, accommodations, plane tickets, day and night entertainment, and other boarding packages. On top of that, a cruise ship should give visitors a comfortable and stress-free holiday. It should provide you with a pleasant experience.

Remember, people, decide to spend their valuable vacation time aboard a sailboat because it provides the utmost in luxury, relaxation, and entertainment.To help you plan your cruise, here are some fundamental procedures and key aspects you need to know to make your trip more pleasurable and receive your money's worth.

• One of the most significant aspects is the destination of cruise ships. Choosing a certain trip location may go a long way in ensuring you get the most out of it. Cruise companies provide different sites in your cruise package. Here are some examples of the most common places individuals intend to sail: Alaska, the Mexico Canal, Panama Island, and the Caribbean.

• Another key element to consider is who you are picking up. Cruise ships have various ships for different reasons. For example, there are family ships where the entire family, children, and adults, can enjoy the trip, or there are even romance-themed cruises where you and your spouse can enjoy romantic meals, dancing, and other activities. . both can.

• Choose the finest cruise lines. Remember, don't select a cruise holiday only based on your budget. Look at the finest cruise lines you can afford and you are guaranteed to receive your money's worth. There are several cruise lines for different sorts of individuals, giving the greatest in fun and excitement.

• The visitor must also decide on the length of the cruises. You won't want to waste your time on vacation when you should be at work rather than on an island worried about what will happen when you arrive. The cruises provide itineraries of varying lengths. There are three to five-day cruise offers, some start on the eighth day and may go up to a month or more. Some cruises provide a four-month tour around the world.

• You should also examine the number of activities on a given cruise. A cruise ship should include basic facilities, such as excellent lodging with private bathrooms. There should also be activities that give the traveler a choice of leisure activities. For example, rock climbing, ice skating, diving, play facilities, swimming pools, gymnasiums, and spas. Cruise operations differ from business to company. Choose the cruise lines that meet your requirements.

• You should also consider shipping from a certain transportation firm. Find out the age of the boat by examining the opening dates or by contacting the firm for a particular boat. If feasible, request a boat tour. Observe the way the employees operate and also notice whether the workers clean.

• Receive a reservation in advance. Booking early means cheaper packages and fewer difficulties securing a cruise. Most cruise companies provide a huge number of discounts if you book several months or more before your trip period. For additional information about a cruise itinerary, check a cruise website.

Cruise lines regularly announce their schedules on their websites and provide online bookings. You may also visit your local cruise travel agency and enquire about cruise lines.

• If you are planning to take shore excursions, always book to prevent frustration and disappointment. Shore excursions are a terrific chance to see other nations and learn about their culture. There are also the greatest shopping choices here.

These are just a few of the guidelines while planning a cruise. If you wish to book a cruise, it is important to contact a travel agency specializing in cruises to receive the best offer available. Travel agents may also function as advisors. Don't be scared to ask questions regarding a certain cruise and what to anticipate.

Cruise Critic - Your one-stop shop for cruise information

If this is your first cruise, you should at least have an understanding of what cruises are all about. Your travel agent just provides you with vacation options or brochures from several cruise lines.

What if you have questions regarding the cruise package offered? What if you want to keep on top of the newest advances in the cruise industry? What will be your credible source of knowledge to answer these questions?

Add Cruise Critic to your favorites today and you will get and learn a lot about cruises. Cruise Critic is an interactive community that was started in 1995. All seasoned and beginner cruise travelers may join our community to discuss their experiences, study, and plan their next or first cruise holiday.

It's a one-stop-shop with all the information you need. Includes a comprehensive itinerary planner for cruises such as the following:

- Latest impartial assessments of trips of 225 ships and more

- Corporate and corporate profile of 55 cruise lines

- Useful information about activities and attractions in more than 135 ports across the globe

- Cruise ratings and reviews based on readers' viewpoint and experience

- various cruise packages

- Useful cruise suggestions for early-season cruise travelers

Cruise Critic helps cruise guests select the finest ship for their interests and organize the ideal cruise trip. They also present the latest news and thoughts on the cruise business. Due to its prominence as a trustworthy cruise guide, it is one of the busiest online cruise services with over 160,000 registered users online.

It comprises the following parts to assist cross-checking of the relevant information and details.

- AT YOUR SERVICE section, which covers numerous issues and gives a clear and comprehensive explanation of the standards, in particular, the laws and regulations on board

- BEYOND COVERAGE section which focuses on addressing numerous cruise queries straight from major cruise lines. They also give behind-the-scenes insight into how the cruise ship runs.

- COMMUNITY Zone where individuals share diverse thoughts on cruise lines, cruise packages, and more.

- CRUISE Deals area, which focuses more on the current offers from various cruise lines

• The CRUISE NEWS area offers the latest cruise news and commentary. Updated regularly

• The CRUISE PLANNING area, which contains subjects such as the current cruise trends, various cabin packages, last-minute voyages, and more.

• CRUISE LINE REVIEWS AND PROFILES area. As noted above, it offers ratings of over 225 active cruise lines and profiles of 55 cruise lines.

• CRUISE STYLE sections containing in-depth evaluations, tales, and numerous styles of cruises including:

1. Romance
2. Second family
3. Elderly folks
4. Gays and lesbians
5. Disabled

6. Alone
7. Luxury
8. Smooth adventure
9. Ocean crossings
10. Vacation

• DESTINATION area with detailed profiles of the 20 cruise areas and more than 135 stopovers across the globe.

• The EDITOR'S SELECTION section, which comprises your most significant personal selections and suggestions, as well as your top 10.

• FIND A Trip SECTION where you may pick the cruise that best meets your preferences, whether by location, cruise company, or price.

• LINK EXCHANGE PROGRAM MESSAGE TABLES place where members and guests may submit all their comments, recommendations, and blogs.

• TREND WATCH section addressing numerous themes relating to the cruise industry that have altered or are in transition (such as solo travel or low carb cruises) (such as solo travel or low carb cruises)

Current forecasts of cruise ship reviews

Another element of Cruise Critics is its prognosis for the cruise industry. You do this every first quarter of the year. It also helps cruise industry executives prepare for the future. Here are some of Cruise Critic's newest predictions for 2006.

• Thanks to family packages introduced in past years, cruises became perfect holidays for families.

• Boats without a complete children's program will have trouble managing hundreds of enthusiastic youngsters.

• Traditional swimming pools will presently go out of favor. The new focus of attention is the onboard water park.

• Don't be startled when Ronald McDonald meets you on board. Cruise companies continue to integrate prominent brands into cruise lines, restaurants, and dining locations.

• Due to the rise in cruise ship equipment, cruise fares are projected to increase.

• There are more pending cruise destinations and Cunard Lines Queen Mary 2 will travel around the globe. More and more will happen each year, so remain tuned to Cruise Critic, your one-stop shop for cruise information.

Find the greatest cruise deals

The tourism sector has been a big asset on various continents for numerous years. They leverage their natural riches to attract tourists, notably cruise passengers. Travel is becoming one of its primary sources of investment.

Cruise companies took the tourism sector by storm last season. In reality, according to data on the number of cruise passengers visiting the country, between 8 and 9 million passengers have taken use of luxury cruise lines. This is solely the 2005 record. Despite the luxury and pricey value of the trip, many Americans still desire to engage in this activity. Industry experts predict the number of travelers to double this year. Cruise operators are already thinking about new itineraries and vacation packages they might offer guests for this year's trips. A modification must be done so that the passengers may feel fresh emotions and enthusiasm.

Cruise ships are also encountering strong competition. More than a cruise, it provides the greatest shopping possibilities and lowest costs. They worry about having their manner of treating travelers. Since most passengers don't care about value anymore, you may provide them a luxury vacation anytime they find it comfortable.

Reality reveals that January, February, and March are the finest months to sail. This is termed the "wave period" for cruise ships. They love this sort since it may add to the adventure of the trip. Big waves move cruise ships. It raises your adrenaline. In addition, it was also the months of January to March that garnered the greatest reservations last year. Sales also climbed by 35 percent, which is roughly half of the additional profit they had. In peak season, it is a fantastic opportunity to take advantage of the greatest cruise bargains.

Businesses naturally seek to compete with each other for each passenger that crosses their way. This is also the season when they offer their finest bargains. Each cruise company has its tactics. Some provide passenger rewards, additional beverages, blackberries, and occasionally phones. This is expressly justified for certain packages.

Make sure you have enough time to make a selection while browsing for the cruise line. This will help you locate the cruise company that fits all of your customers' demands. You may also peruse newspapers and magazines and search the travel website for top firms that promote unique benefits, such as special discounts. Those who do not wish to read paper advertising may browse online.

Search online for the website of these firms. You can get all the information you need on their websites. Most of the main cruise lines have their websites. Immediately after picking your desired cruise line, you may immediately make a call. Be sure to mention your name, age, and state of residence. You may also open up to them, whether you are traveling alone or in a group.

It's also more advantageous to let them know that you made your prior journey on their cruise line. Some firms provide specific grants to this state. This is also included in their cruise offerings. All of these elements may help you earn higher discounts.

Sometimes it is more helpful to have a direct touch with the agents. You know more about the positives and negatives that you need to pay attention to. They are also more aware of the specifics of the cruise company. A competent agency can provide you with the greatest cruise you are searching for. With the rivalry that also exists in recruiting customers, agents labor hard before they can achieve a lot with the client. They may give you fewer consulting rates than the corporation does.

Chapter -4

Choose the cruise lines that are perfect for you

Is Cruise Vacation Right For You?
Where should you go?
Which cruises are perfect for you?

A lot of individuals have varied questions concerning cruises. Some individuals cannot determine whether a cruise trip is good for them or their families. Others don't know which cruise lines to choose and others don't know where to travel. First, you need to determine whether a cruise holiday is good for you and your family. At the outset, anybody may embark on a cruise. All you have to do is select the cruise that's appropriate for you.

Ask yourself this question,
what are you searching for on a specific vacation?
Is it peaceful and relaxed, romantic, full of events, parties, or whatever?

Choose the one you like. Once you've determined what to do on a cruise, it's simple to select the ideal one for you. Ask your local cruise travel agent about the different packages provided by cruise companies or ask friends who have taken a cruise on their vacation. You also need to know the various sorts of cruises. Many sorts of cruises are adapted to the requirements and interests of each individual. There are luxury cruises that provide top-notch services that may equal those of five-star hotels on land.

You may also embark on exploration cruises, where cruise companies offer voyages to areas like the Amazon, the Galapagos Islands, and other eccentric spots. Some cruises provide journeys to multiple ports of call in various countries. Here you may experience diverse cultures from different nations that your cruise will visit.

Family cruises are also provided. This style of a cruise is suited for individuals traveling as a family, particularly with youngsters. These cruises provide a mix of aboard and onshore activities ideal for adults and children. They provide particular packages for youngsters so that they constantly have something to do and don't become bored or concerned.

These numerous sorts of cruises are accessible on the market. You should find one where everyone can rest and enjoy. It is also vital to pick the cruise line where you wish to spend your holiday. There are aspects to consider while selecting a cruise. Here are a few:

• Price: Find out how much you can pay for a cruise. Cruise rates differ from one cruise line to another. If you want a first-class cruise, be prepared to pay a lot of money. Some ships offer economy class which might save you money on a voyage.

• Itineraries: You should also know where the cruise is heading. Reaching the places of your choice will help you optimize your leisure and pleasure on your cruise trip. Cruises provide a range of places; You need to select the lens that works best for you.

• Passengers: Cruise lines attract various sorts of passengers. It's crucial to choose the sorts of individuals you want to spend time with to mingle better and have more fun.

All this information is accessible from a travel agent. However, it is also accessible on the Internet. Using the Internet to gather information on a certain cruise is considerably more convenient and you can simply compare practically any sort of trip.

The Internet also provides articles published by various individuals about their thoughts on certain cruise holidays. You may base your selection on publications and websites alone, but where to go is always up to you. The Internet also provides online reservation services. You may simply make a reservation online with a cruise company.

You should also select a cruise company that provides an optimal timetable that meets your preferences. Some voyages take just three days for extended trips around the globe of more than four months. select the one that fits you best. Remember that picking the cruises and cruise lines you will be traveling on may also be a deciding element in the enjoyment you experience. So you need to find the correct one that can fulfill or even surpass your expectations. Don't make your cruise trip rely on pricing alone. Enjoying your cruise holiday, despite the expense, is your primary goal.

Cruise comments: what to anticipate from a cruise

Vacation implies getting rid of anger and stress. It is crucial to consider getaways that help you to let go of these problems. We were never weary of driving a hundred kilometers only to rest in one area. You won't have to worry about big baggage. It's the holidays. If you want a vacation full of alternatives, try taking a cruise. Whether you've never been there and you're not sure if it would be right for you, read on. The solution to your doubts is here.

This post does not support or promote any one cruise company, it merely offers you an overview of what various businesses are providing. This comprises the cruise locations, the different pricing packages, and the services provided. Before the voyage, cruise companies often arrange pre-cruise treats. Includes travelers who remain a few days at the site of departure and engage in a guided trip.

For example, if your starting location is in Los Angeles, you may visit renowned spots like Hollywood and Venus Beach. On the day of your voyage, you will be taken to the pier where your cruise ship will meet you. It takes roughly 45 minutes to check in your bags and board the cruise. Your butler will be waiting for you and strangely your baggage is already at your cabin.

Once you've unloaded and arranged your belongings, take a journey onboard the ship. Most cruise lines offer huge balconies so you may stroll outdoors. You may enjoy numerous minutes of relaxation at the spa. If you wish to be in excellent health on board, a gym with weight equipment is at your disposal. Onboard, there are swimming pools for adults and children. Sunbeds and seats are also available if you wish to watch your children having fun in the pool.

Entertainment is also offered throughout your boat holiday. A state-of-the-art theater is offered for onboard entertainment. Various entertainment, such as Hollywood blockbusters and children's shows, is up for grabs. If you are searching for a different sort of entertainment, there are various themed pubs and a nightclub with live music that remains up until the early hours of the morning. If you wish to try your luck, there is an onboard casino that provides a range of games, exactly like Las Vegas.

If you miss your shopping habit every week, there is also a mall where you may find personal things and other items you might need aboard. Libraries and leisure facilities are also great if you're wanting to read books or stay up with the newest business and sports news. Cafes are available 24 hours a day to serve travelers who desire peaceful talk.

Grocery shopping is one of the main services given by cruise companies. The top chefs from various countries are chosen to produce and serve exceptional delicacies so that your dining experience aboard is genuinely unique. There are formal dining rooms with strict dress requirements. Food is provided especially: first-class gourmet service. If you're searching for informal eating, there are also bars, cafés, and pizzas on board, which are normally open for longer hours for meals. All of these dishes are included in the cruise fees. Cruise itineraries often involve stops at various ports every alternate day, depending on the itinerary of the cruise company you are traveling with.

You have the choice of remaining aboard the ship or disembarking to join other guests on a guided tour. You may also explore each stopover on your own, as long as you come back to the ship by the planned departure time. Booking a cruise is simple. Use the services of a travel agency or register on the official website of a certain cruise company.

You may find information about trip places and cruise packages at inexpensive pricing. There are also discounts and special deals for travelers. With this cruise review, you won't overlook it if you are going on your first cruise holiday.

What to look for on a cruise

Cruises are one of the most popular forms of holiday nowadays. Individuals are contemplating taking cruise holidays because of the relaxation for all the various sorts of people it provides. There is a large selection of cruises and cruise lines out there, you need to pick one that meets your preferences. How would you feel if you travel and rested at the same time? While cruising, they offer all the luxuries that would gratify any sort of individual. There are also many sorts of cruise packages to select from with different locations and specializations.

You may choose a family cruise package that entertains adults and youngsters. There are also Singles Cruises that provide dating and other activities ideal for singles. There are also cruise packages for couples. Here you and your companion may enjoy days of romantic meals, dancing, and other entertainment and activities.

Some folks look through a lot of cruise company brochures but still don't know anything about the voyage and the ship itself. They frequently don't know what sort of cruise to take or where to go. Cruises differ based on the cruise company. They have many stopovers and different brands of cruise ships. Others have swimming pools and some don't. You need to know which cruise to take and what sort of cruise lines a certain cruise company provides.

For most people, a cruise ship is a big white ocean liner that is filled with pleasure and leisure. They all have various sorts of gadgets and services and come in varying sizes. There are cruise lines that specialize in providing a romantic, family-friendly trip with amenities and entertainment for the entire family. It entertains adults, teens, and even tiny toddlers. Other cruise lines provide a customized voyage for holidaymakers who cannot afford luxury ships. Of course, there are other cruises geared for maximum luxury and comfort.

Some cruise companies feature gymnasiums on board that can rival any indoor gymnasium available. It has all the required equipment to provide you with appropriate instruction. There are also thermal boats on board that provide beauty treatments, massages, and other services that you would find at a conventional spa.

Various cruise lines provide many services and activities aboard their cruise lines to compete with each other and attract more consumers. Climbing equipment is also available to experience the joy and thrill of rock climbing. You may also conduct your morning one-mile jog using a jogging track on board. Entertainment amenities are also provided by most major cruise companies. You may view movies at an onboard cinema, see plays, watch concerts, and even participate in game shows. If you wish to be married on a cruise, there are cruise lines that provide this option.

There are accommodations to suit all cruise budgets. You may pick an economy class with smaller accommodations or first-class cabins with butler service. Many cruise companies include casinos into their cruise lines so that adults may experience a Vegas-style casino with all the games accessible in one. There are games like poker, craps, roulette, and even slot machines. Who knows? Maybe you can recuperate what you spent on your trip.

Today, numerous cruise companies amuse youngsters. They provide services that can satisfy the demands of your kid. It includes activities such as face painting, games, video games, galleries, and areas exclusively created for children of all ages. Whatever style of cruise you like; Cruises are always a unique experience for travelers. It distracts you from the hustle and bustle of daily life and all you would think about is how to relax on a cruise every day.

Remember, while picking a cruise or company, you shouldn't only focus on pricing. You should remember that the holidays are for relaxing and forgetting about worries and worry. Choose a cruise holiday that is persuasive not only in terms of pricing but also in terms of the amenities and services of a specific cruise ship.

The past, present, and future voyage

Consider treating yourself and your family to a deluxe cruise trip. On a set departure day, travel on one of these first-class hotel-style cruises for the duration of your holiday. Serve as a sailboat, temporary home, retail mall, massage parlor, entertainment facility, etc.

A cruise ship can accommodate all of these and additional services in an urban environment. Yes, he can. Not only does this make a cruise a wonderful experience, but also a terrific alternative for your next holiday.

Cruises, often known as cruise ships or luxury cruises, are passenger ships used for recreational travel. The travel itself and the services on board are a vital component of the cruise experience. The fast expansion of the cruise sector in the tourism industry has pushed cruise companies to construct new ships to fulfill the demands of the expanding number of cruise passengers. It offers itineraries to transatlantic places where engineers and sailors have devised trips capable of withstanding diverse sea circumstances.

History and development

The iconic Titanic is now one of the progenitors of cruise ships and is home to outstanding restaurants, well-appointed accommodations, and other facilities guests require on board. At the end of the 19th century, Albert Ballin, director of the Hamburg-America Line, was the first to consistently send his transatlantic ships on extended excursions south through the harshest winter weather of the North Atlantic. Others followed and created customized boats capable of withstanding summer and winter sailing conditions.

Other cruise destinations have been offered, such as the Caribbean and Mediterranean islands. Newer ships have consequently been developed to handle voyages in these places. Not just as a ship but also as an advertisement for a cruise trip. The Love Boat is a 1970s television series, starring Pacific Princess, the Princess cruise liner. He promoted awareness of cruise travel as a holiday choice not just for the rich but also for average people in the United States.

Cruises now

In 2004, there were several hundred cruise ships with a carrying capacity of over 3,000 people and handling of over 100,000 tonnes. This makes her the biggest ship ever constructed. You can reach places as far as Antarctica. Modern ships are also regarded as "floating hotels" with complete personnel in addition to the typical cruise ship employees. These boats are also built to offer an appropriate amount of food. Cruise ships provide thousands of meals in all places.

The storage facilities for raw materials and drinks are provided with the most current storage technology. Cruise guests may eat more food and drink over a typical seven-day vacation. For example, guests and employees aboard Royal Caribbean International's Mariner of the Seas ship may devour 20,000 pounds of steak, 28,000 eggs, 8,000 liters of ice cream, and 18,000 pieces of pizza in a week.

The Queen Mary 2 is presently the biggest vessel in service. It has 151,400 gross tonnages and is owned by Cunard Line, a part of Carnival Corporation, now the biggest cruise line. This British cruiser is 1,132 feet long, 236 feet high, and can transport 2,620 people. It is capable of traversing the North Atlantic at a pace of 30 knots.

Queen Mary 2 boasts five onboard pools, a curving stairway, a ballroom, a 360-degree promenade, and various specialized stores. It was created to reignite the draw of ocean liners, whose industry nearly collapsed as jet travel started to gain importance on the Atlantic route.

Cruise of the future

Recently, on February 6, 2006, Royal Caribbean International stated that it will launch the world's biggest and most costly cruise ship in the autumn of 2009 with an estimated price tag of $ 1.24 billion. It is named Proyecto Génesis, which can also carry up to 6,400 people. It is projected to have a registered gross ton of roughly 220,000. A gross tonnage, which is the usual measure of a ship's size, equals 100 cubic feet. The cost of $ 1.24 billion will cover all the changes required to restore the inside of the ship.

What else can you anticipate from these cruises?

Do you enjoy cruises? If you are a lover of clean and stylish cruise lines, 2006 has its fresh assortment of cruise lines. Chances are you will discover six new cruise lines on a cruise ship to fill your 2006 voyage. If you think this is a nice cruise review, think again! We only provide you with the advantage of advanced information for your cruise plans for the year. Well, what are you waiting for? Here are the six main cruise lines with their newest voyages.

1. Holland America Noordam Cruise Ship: This brand new Holland America ship was inaugurated on February 22nd. It would also be Holland America's final Vista-class cruiser. However, it is the first to be designed for the cruise line's Signature of Excellence program. For this reason, this cruise review looks to be a first in recent years. The Noordam has a capacity of 1,848 people. There are design enhancements on this new cruise ship for additional pleasure and enjoyment for cruise ship passengers. The architectural upgrades have mostly concentrated on the common rooms and cabins, the gathering spot for many cruise guests.

There are other expansions, including the famed Exploration Café. As cruise ship guests know, this is an internet cafe/cafe, gaming area, and library. The New York Times runs the whole Exploration Café. Noordam's debut season in 2006 consisted of winter cruises from New York to the Caribbean.

2. NCL America's Pride of Hawaii: This new 2006 NCL America cruise is the sister ship of Norwegian Jewel. For the maritime corporation, Pride of Hawaii is the first new build from the hull. The start will take place in June. This liner is planned to accommodate 2,224 people. This is the next phase in NCL America's "Freestyle Cruising" philosophy. The inside of Pride of Hawaii will, of course, be Hawaiian. This tour will sail weekly on Mondays and touch the islands that occupy Honolulu.

3. Royal Caribbean Freedom of the Seas: This new 2006 cruise ship will be unveiled in May. This 158,000-tonne cruise ship has a capacity of 3,600 people. It will be 10,000 tonnes bigger than Cunard's Queen Mary 2. This should make her the biggest cruise ship of 2006. Freedom of the Seas will feature new and upgraded facilities for the delight of guests. There is already ongoing talk regarding the function of the surf park among cruise ship tourists.

We also anticipate hot tubs to protrude on the side of this magnificent voyage. Another innovation, the H2O zone may potentially become a practical success for travelers. After its debut, Freedom of the Seas will sail on seven-day Caribbean cruises from Miami.

4. The Crown Princess of New Princess Cruises: This gorgeous new cruise is planned to start in June. To the delight of cruise ship passengers in 2006, the Crown Princess is projected to accommodate 3,110 cruise ship passengers.

5. The new cruise line, Princess Cruises, has remodeled Skywalker's Disco, which has acquired popularity among cruise lines of its other cruise lines. They also have the Lotus Spa and wonderful news for everyone. It has been expanded in Crown Princess!

New pastries and sandwiches will grace the International Café. Crown Princess will include the cruise line's first fish and wine bar. Other notable restaurants such as the Wheelhouse Bar, Sabatini's Trattoria, and Sterling Steakhouse have flourished. The Crown Princess will be making a round journey from the Red Hook station in New York City. It will make stops in the Eastern Caribbean and Bermuda and the Turks & Caicos Islands.

6. MSC Musica: MSC will debut their new 2006 cruise ship very late in the year on July 1st. Music is an Italian ship that will propel MSC into the ranks of the major cruise companies. It should accommodate 2,550 people. One of its primary features will be that 80 percent of its 1,275 staterooms will be overseas. In addition, 65 percent of these cabins feature a patio. There will also be a huge wellness area. Passengers on musical cruises will also have many eateries. You will also enjoy a three-story waterfall and many additional entertainment alternatives. The music will spread over the eastern Mediterranean from Venice.

7. CostaConcordia by Costa Cruises: this modern cruise ship constructed in 2006 is owned by Carnival Corporation, situated in Italy. It will be the biggest cruise ship in the Costa Cruises fleet. It will also start functioning rather late this year, on July 14. It should have a capacity of 3,000 passengers. To inspire its passengers, CostaConcordia will feature a European architectural motif for the interiors. All room names will be influenced or focused towards Europe.

You will have the Grand Bar Berlin, the Cafeteria Helsinki, and the Milan and Rome dining rooms. If you are seeking entertaining things to do while boating, CostaConcordia provides a Formula 1 driving simulator for fans.

Are you hopping eagerly when it starts? This new cruise ship will sail all year round in the Western Mediterranean. You will proceed to the port of Civitavecchia in Rome. Are you already confused? Check out additional cruise reviews from these new cruise lines to find out where your 2006 cruise will be.

Chapter -5

What are some of the greatest closed-loop cruise itineraries?

Fort Lauderdale to Bahamas, Mexico, and Grand Cayman: Cruise from Fort Lauderdale aboard the spectacular Celebrity Edge, one of the most inventive and stunning ships afloat, destined for the Bahamas and the warm, blue seas of the Caribbean. You'll spend a day in colorful Nassau, on New Providence Island, with plenty of opportunities to explore the powder-sand beaches, snorkel over beautiful reefs, browse for crafts at the Straw Market, or experience an adrenaline rush on one of the huge water slides at the luxurious Atlantis Resort.

After a day at sea to enjoy the ship and its spectacular Resort Deck, you'll arrive at Puerto Costa Maya, Mexico. A huge assortment of alternatives awaits here, such as calm tubing at the pristine Bacalar Lagoon, where you'll flow over cenote-fed water that's an amazing hue of blue. Or you may try rafting, sail-and-snorkel trips, and even a healing session with a real shaman. There's Mayan history here, too, at the Chacchoben Ruins, a short drive from the harbor.

From Cozumel, you might take an expedition to the stunning Mayan ruins at Tulum set against a background of the blue sea. Try a salsa and margarita-making session, or sail a glass-bottomed kayak over rainbow-colored reefs. This seven-night trip is also named Grand Cayman, where you can witness gorgeous white beaches, pristine reefs, and uncommon animal encounters, including swimming with stingrays in the warm, shallow waters of Stingray City.

Los Angeles to the Mexican Riviera : Sail round-trip from Los Angeles to the gorgeous Mexican Riviera aboard the freshly renovated Celebrity Millennium. From busy Puerto Vallarta, you may take a whale-watching trip, peruse the arty boutiques, or sit back at the beach to enjoy the soft sand and blue waves of the Pacific.

At Cabo San Lucas, there's more whale-watching along the untamed, rocky shore, or activities ranging from kayaking to snorkeling. Explore the Art District and historic adobe houses in neighboring San Jose del Cabo, or explore the Baja desert on a 4×4 off-road adventure.

From Ensenada, you may dive over underwater rock formations at Todos Santos island, or take a wine-tasting excursion to Calafia Valley, Mexico's wine-growing area. Closer to port, enjoy a walking tour of the cosmopolitan metropolis to try tequila and tacos.

You'll have three full days at sea on this tour to soak in the Pacific sunshine and enjoy Celebrity Millennium. Why not upgrade to The Retreat for a genuine sense of luxury? You'll enjoy a magnificent suite and eat in the gorgeous, fine dining Luminae restaurant, reserved for guests of this secluded enclave.

Seattle to Alaska, the Inside Passage, and Dawes Glacier: Spend seven nights discovering the natural grandeur of Alaska aboard Celebrity Solstice, the ideal ship for such magnificent scenery, with her plenty of outdoor space and top-deck Lawn Club. You'll visit picturesque Ketchikan, from where you may take a bear-spotting excursion, try kayaking, join an expedition to fish for king crab, or simply enjoy the colorful town.

Next, there's a whole day gently sailing the 30-mile Endicott Arm Fjord, through gushing waterfalls and pieces of floating ice that has broken off the majestic Dawes Glacier, a 600-foot tall wall of blue-white ice. The view of this massive river of ice meets the sea is a highlight of the day. You'll also explore Juneau, the best site for whale-watching, hiking, and exhilarating flightseeing adventures over snow-covered mountains. In Skagway, you'll get the opportunity to ride the majestic White Pass and Yukon Route train, climbing high over steep passes, following the track of tough prospectors from the Gold Rush days.

While Celebrity Solstice goes back to Seattle, there's a day aboard to relax as the ship makes its way through the small passageways of the Inside Passage, past wooded islands and rock-strewn beaches, with wonderful prospects for observing whales and bears from your vantage position on deck. There's also a stop at ancient Victoria on Canada's Vancouver Island, where you can see a delightful combination of exquisite, British colonial buildings, smart boutiques, and craft breweries before you return to Seattle.

Fort Lauderdale to Puerto Rico, St. Thomas, and St. Kitts: Sail to the sun aboard Celebrity Apex, leaving Fort Lauderdale, Florida for colorful Puerto Rico, where an afternoon and evening in port mean you'll witness two sides of flamboyant San Juan. Explore the massive stronghold, Castillo San Felipe del Morro, and the vividly colored streets of Old San Juan, or visit the Bacardi distillery to learn about and try the famed rum. You'll discover lots of military history in St. Kitts, notably the rough Brimstone Hill Fortress, a large fortress established by the British in 1690. This little island packs a huge punch, with an immense range of things to do.

Trundle through the sugarcane fields on a picturesque train excursion, or explore Mount Liamuiga, a dormant volcano in the island's heart. Learn how to create your own delicious truffles at a chocolate class.

Visit nearby Nevis and visit the birthplace of Alexander Hamilton, one of the founding fathers of the U.S.

At Charlotte Amalie, St. Thomas, you'll find it impossible to resist exploring the crystal-clear water via snorkeling, kayaking, or sailboat. For a day sunning on the lovely Honeymoon Beach, the verdant, low-key island of St. John is an easy hop over the ocean.

Fort Lauderdale to Key West, Belize, and Grand Cayman: Set sail from Fort Lauderdale aboard the brand new Celebrity Apex, the second in Celebrity Cruises' award-winning Edge line. You'll spend a day in quirky, colorful Key West, where you can try stand-up paddleboarding or take a bicycle tour through the palm-lined streets of this joyfully offbeat city. Explore Ernest Hemingway's old house, and don't miss a chance to eat the island's famed key lime pie.

Tropical Belize is all with excitement, from cave tubing to ziplining high above the jungle canopy. Mayan treasures have been absorbed by the jungle, making their setting even more spectacular. Visit mystical Lamanai, one of Mesoamerica's greatest ceremonial sites, or enjoy a tour of the ancient hilltop remains of Xunantunich and the temple of El Castillo.

This trip also visits the seaside paradise of Cozumel, for all manner of activities, shopping, and hot Mexican food. There's even a chance to attend a taco-making workshop. Celebrity Apex then sets a course east to the island of Grand Cayman, famous for its gorgeous beaches and marine life, such as the gentle stingrays that cluster on the Stingray City sandbar waiting to be fed morsels of squid.

You'll have one more day at sea to soak up the tropical sun on the deck and enjoy the numerous delights of the ship. Lounge at the Magic Carpet with a beverage; this multifunctional platform is cantilevered over the side of the ship, with water on three sides, so you'll feel as though you are flying. Or rest in the green tranquillity of Eden, or eat al fresco in the magnificent Rooftop Garden Grill.

Cape Liberty to Bermuda: Charge your champagne glass and raise a toast to Lady Liberty on this seven-night trip from Cape Liberty, New Jersey to stylish Bermuda and back. As your ship, Celebrity Summit edges out of the dock, you'll get wonderful views of the Manhattan skyline as you sail straight past the Statue of Liberty and then out under the renowned Verrazzano-Narrows Bridge, setting course south-east to sunny Bermuda.

Here, on this enchanting island where the beach is pink and the policeman wears knee-length shorts, you'll have two and a half days to explore, which means two overnight stays.

There's much to do, from snorkeling to golf, touring the shops and galleries in Hamilton, the pastel-hued capital, and seeing the island's forts. Hike the historic Railway Trail, consisting of 18 miles of picturesque route following the length of an ancient railroad line.

Set sail on a catamaran tour after sunset, or join a pub crawl of Hamilton's establishments after dark. One of the most distinctive things to do in Bermuda is to enjoy a Black 'n' Stormy, the potent local specialty composed of dark rum with ginger beer and a slice of lime.

Chapter -6

16 Cruise Tips for First-Timers

When planning for your first cruise, one of the most critical tools is communication–with your travel mates as well as with the cruise company. From getting to know the priorities and interests of your friends or family coming along to understanding the opportunities and activities available during your sailing, there is so much to learn (such as knowing the difference between port vs starboard) and get excited about before you even set sail.

Follow these cruise guidelines for first-timers to guarantee that your first cruise holiday is all you wish it to be and so much more.

1: Pack smart : One of the finest pieces of cruise advice for first-timers is not to overpack. The secret to optimizing both the space in your bag and in your cabin comes down to utilizing travel gadgets that accomplish the double purpose. For example, a toiletry kit that stores all your personal hygiene and beauty things may sit on the vanity and take up room, but selecting for one that folds out and hangs by a hook means freeing up that space.

Toss a few hook magnets into your backpack to serve as extra wardrobe hangers in your cabin, because the doors are metal. They're also perfect for hanging your SeaPass card lanyard or a smart swimwear coverup.

2: Consider a longer itinerary : While weekend cruises are popular and regarded as a wonderful way to try cruising, long-time cruisers would argue that they're significantly different from itineraries of a week or more. On longer excursions, you'll have the chance to completely relax and enjoy both the ship and her locations.

3: Back up your gadgets : In the days before your trip, relocate extra data on your phone, laptops, and camera memory cards to an external hard drive or, at the absolute least, sync the photographs and data to a cloud-based service so that you have the space necessary for recording all the memories you are about to create. The last thing you want to do is miss the sunset from your balcony because you have to navigate through your gadgets attempting to erase old images to make place for new ones—especially if it's your first time on a cruise.

4: Double-check your data plan : The impulse to share your holiday images of stunning Caribbean beaches and selfies shot at historic locations is fantastic, but if you are outside of your nation and your data plan is limiting, that sharing might cost a big fortune. Before commencing your cruise holiday, verify your mobile phone data plan to learn of its limits and additional expenses or, preferably, the absence of them.

5: Understand credit card fees : The same cruise advice for first-timers applies to your credit cards, too. Many firms charge a percentage for overseas transactions, while others don't impose this cost at all. It may not make a difference when buying a few postcards to ship back home, but when your memento is a handmade rug or a unique bottle of an old rum, the international transaction tax may be unpleasant.

6: Wear the clothing you seldom wear at home : One surprise cruise suggestion for first-timers is to pack the outfits that generally remain at the back of your wardrobe. These costumes may be "too much" for your usual routine, but a cruise trip surely isn't your everyday. With the range of experiences, you may have in just one day—from breakfast to poolside leisure, and from onshore excursions to gourmet dining onboard—there is so much potential to express your personality.

Rest confident that your other travelers will, too. Cruises are a wonderful location for expression, and being at sea brings out a person's enthusiasm and creativity.

7: Start a group chat : If you've booked your voyage more than a few months ahead, take advantage of that early planning time by setting up a fun cruise discussion with your travel mates. You'll all want to be on the same page regarding activity priorities at each port before you board the cruise.

For example, if snorkeling in gorgeous, clear water is something everyone wants to do, you may agree on the port you'd want to select for a snorkel tour, and then book it when reservations open to snag your position. Many shore excursions are available for advance booking, and popular selections will fill up, so it is best not to be exploring the alternatives aboard while seasoned cruisers have had their top-choice excursions planned for months.

8: Research your ports in advance : If your pre-cruise preparations don't give much time to read up on the places along your route, there is a simple way to prepare to appreciate the best they offer. Plan to attend the onboard destination lectures which are normally presented the day before arrival at the port.

One of the ship's locations experts will outline what cuisine, activities, mementos, and experiences are definitely not-to-miss, while also presenting some of the history, geography, and predicted weather of the destination. Noting down what interests you have and what ideas you gather from the presentation can help you determine what excursions to plan, while also offering you hints on how to arrange your day to make the most of your time in each place.

9: Protect yourself from the sun : Throwing a container of sunscreen into your suitcase is an easy decision (particularly when contemplating what to pack for a Caribbean cruise) (especially when planning what to pack for a Caribbean cruise). Since your cruise will take you to a number of ports, you'll want to be armed with several kinds of sun protection.

Add UV-blocking sunglasses to your basics, and consider buying for UVA- and UVB-blocking apparel to wear on days when you expect to be out in the sun for numerous hours. Swimwear and sweat-wicking, lightweight adventure apparel are available in fabrics that protect your skin from the sun while keeping you cool and comfortable.

10: Pay attention to arrival and departure times : Of all the cruise guidelines for first-timers, this one is vital to make sure you're really able to join your trip. Always be sure to check the small print of your cruise ticket that contains ship departure and arrival ports. For example, is your ship going from the Port of Miami or Port Everglades in Fort Lauderdale? If you're flying, you'll want to make sure you fly into the city closest to your cruise departure port or ensure transportation is accessible from your airport of choice to the relevant terminal.

Even after you've got your cities selected, there is still the question of the port terminal. Many ships might land at a single port, and it can be tough to order your cab to drive about until you find your ship. Your cruise ticket and contract will indicate the departure terminal, such as Terminal 25 at Port Everglades, which is where you'll find Celebrity Edge homeporting for her Caribbean sailings.

11: Agree on a meet-up site : Whether you are traveling with one spouse or your whole extended family, it is a fantastic idea to agree on one area where you meet up before joint activities or significant meals.

A favorite area aboard Celebrity Edge, for example, is the sailing ship model fashioned of pearl strands on the second of the three-floor martini bar, midship. It is immediately identifiable, close to all elevators and eating locations, and its position in a multi-level bar means that people-watching, while you wait, is added entertainment.

12: Set up your onboard account in advance : The last place you want to spend your first few hours on your maiden cruise is in line to ask questions and set up your onboard spending account at the Guest Relations desk. Circumventing this is surprisingly straightforward and may be done when you check-in for your cruise online or via the app.

Connect your credit card to your onboard account to make shipboard purchases for anything from drinks and specialty dining appointments to shore excursions and spa treatments. Having your account set up beforehand also prevents having to approach the Guest Relations desk after your cruise to pay the debt.

13: Learn the lingo : Speaking like a salty sailor is not essential on a cruise holiday, but knowing some fundamental nautical terminology will be beneficial in navigating the ship. To start, acquaint yourself with directional words like "starboard" (the right side of the ship); "port" (the left side); "fore" (towards the bow/front of the ship); "aft" (towards the stern/back of the ship); and "midships," (midway between the front and rear of the ship) (midway between the front and back of the ship).

14: Focus on your wellbeing : Long-term cruisers know that being at sea is the best time and location for concentrating on yourself to come home refocused, balanced, and well-rested. Cruise ships may be renowned for fun in the sun and their large dining selections, but today's ships also have outstanding spas and fitness facilities that provide visitors the equipment, training options, and programs they need to stretch out and work out, relax and re-calibrate. The best approach to discover what health choices your ship has to offer is to visit the spa and wellness center on the first full day when the treatment therapists and personal trainers are available for inquiries and consultations.

15: Stay up late and get up early : Plan to have one truly late night and one early morning—but not one immediately after the other. Being at sea on a cruise is a particular experience, and the changing weather is a crucial aspect of it. To properly admire the ocean's myriad hues as it reflects the sky, take a walk on deck with a cup of coffee or tea as the sun peaks over the horizon to start a new day. Breathe deeply, relish the moment, and set your objectives for another fantastic day.

Nighttime at sea is another chance to experience a special period of introspection. With the stars overhead and the air caressing your skin, the rest of the world and its concerns melt away, allowing room for self-reflection. Or, you may dress up and enjoy your cruise nightlife alternatives.

16: Prepare to meet new pals : Being outside your native environment, and particularly having the unique experience of being out at sea, has the pleasurable impact of physically and metaphorically extending your horizons. Barriers are shattered and shields are let down, and suddenly you are having a heart-to-heart with someone who becomes your new closest friend.

You would have never met if it had not been for this delightful trip, but now you are making plans to do it over again next year (or even sooner) (or even sooner). Sharing social media accounts or email addresses is simplest, but never underestimate the romance and whimsy of sending handwritten letters.

Chapter :7

When Is the Most Appropriate Time to Book a Cruise?

You've chosen a cruise holiday location, such as the sun-warmed Caribbean islands, where you can relax on powdered white-sand beaches and drink icy pia Coladas, or Alaska, where you can watch pods of whales play and witness ice-blue glaciers lose their snowy sides with a huge dramatic scream.

You know what time of year you want to go, and you've even studied what to bring and which shore excursions to plan, but you're not sure when to book your cruise. Find out when is the optimum time to book the cruise itinerary you're thinking about to guarantee your cruise holiday is flawless from the start.

How far ahead of time should you plan a cruise?
Popular cruise itineraries and sailings during peak vacation seasons may rapidly sell out, so you should book as soon as the cruise date is released. Also, when promotional pricing and offers are published, they tend to sell out rapidly, so you should book as soon as you see them.

If you wish to spend the holidays on a cruise, want certain cabin accommodations, especially suites, have a special event to commemorate, and want specialized dining reservations, or want premier spa treatments such as couples massages, book your cruise itinerary as soon as possible. Many cruises are available for booking two years or more before the departure date.

Is it best to plan a cruise as soon as possible or as late as possible?
It's common to hear that the optimum time to book a cruise is either very early or very late in the booking window - that is, from the time a cruise itinerary is announced and around six weeks before the voyage leaves. Each has advantages and disadvantages, so you must decide which is the best option for you.

What are the advantages of booking a cruise in advance?
When you book your cruise early, you have two advantages: a lower price and first choice of rooms, shore excursions, and meal hours. In general, the first quoted price will be the best price for that voyage. When the ship's cabins begin to fill, the cruise price tends to rise, and it may not fall if the voyage is in great demand.

Celebrity's Best Price Guarantee ensures that if a lower cruise price is discovered or promotional cruise pricing is offered after you book, and your booking falls within specific restrictions, the lower cost will be applied to your ticket. When you book early, you get additional first-choice options of various crucial onboard amenities, such as:

Best Options for Lodging
Booking early ensures that you have the most options for staterooms. When you plan a cruise, unlike a hotel reservation, you do not just reserve a cabin category. You may (and should) choose your precise stateroom when making your reservation. Choose the finest stateroom first, then examine the deck plans for your ship to find the ideal position. Suites on every cruise can sell out quickly, as can the most desired locations, such as mid-ship staterooms (which are closer to the main dining rooms, many of the lounges, and have less noticeable movement); top decks (where you'll get a bird's-eye view from your veranda and closer proximity to the pool and sundeck); and one side versus the other of the ship (on certain sailings, this may be important for the view).

Main Dining Room Preferred Times

By booking early, you may also secure your chosen eating hour in the ship's Main Dining Room by selecting the Celebrity Select Dining option. This allows you to eat earlier or later each day, rather than at a regular hour. Early seatings are often booked first, so if you enjoy dining at the same time every evening, scheduling early provides you the greatest chance of obtaining your favorite time, as well as the extra advantage of a more customized dining experience by having the same table and wait for staff each evening.

Make a reservation for popular shore excursions and onboard activities.

When you book your cruise early, you'll have direct access to the wide range of shore activities available on Celebrity Cruises, many of which sell out rapidly. For example, on one of our Hubbard Glacier cruises, there are just a few spaces available for a fantastic small-vessel excursion that brings you up up and personal with Alaska's incredible native animals, breathtaking waterfalls, and the gorgeous glacier situated along the ship's fjord path. Early booking also allows you to secure specialized restaurant dates and hours, as well as set up spa and fitness center appointments before the most popular times and places are taken.

Cancellation Policy for Early Bookings

If buying a cruise a year or more in the future seems overwhelming, rest assured that most Cruises itineraries offer cancellation policies that enable you to cancel your ticket up to 90 days before departing, and as long as you cancel within the stipulated timeframe, you will not be charged the cruise cost.

Chapter -8

When Is the Best Time to Travel by Cruise Ship?

If you're planning your perfect vacation, the optimum time to go on a cruise is when you can balance travel with weather and the availability of the activities and places that most excite you. These are the finest dates to take a trip all over the globe, from hot summers in the Mediterranean to winter retreats in the Southern Hemisphere.

This article includes the following sections:

Alaska: The months of May through September are ideal for a cruise to Alaska. Alaska has a definite peak season when excursions are most easily available, shops are open and energy is strong, and many of the main water viewing activities (such as whale watching) are available.

Summer in Alaska is also peak salmon fishing season for King, Sockeye, and Silver salmon, so you can expect to eat some of the greatest wood-grilled, wild Alaskan salmon you've ever had.

Because many animals go into hiding or hibernation during the winter, the months of May through September provide the greatest chances for wildlife sightings. Keep your eyes open and your camera ready for guillemots, bald eagles, moose, harbor seals, mountain goats, and bears out and about throughout your Alaska cruise, whether you're within a national park or just outside a bar in Ketchikan.

Caribbean: The Caribbean is a popular destination for cruise ships all year. You may enjoy activities like discovering an ancient Mayan ceremonial site in Belize, glass-bottom kayaking above beautiful corals in Bonaire or going for a sail on the turquoise seas around the island of St. Vincent whether you cruise the Eastern, Western, or Southern Caribbean.

The dry season runs from November to April, and these months are characterized by incredibly clear days when practically any plans you make are unlikely to be thwarted by the weather. As a result, the dry season is one of the greatest periods to visit the beautiful Caribbean islands.

From May to October, short rainstorms are common, and while they may send diners at alfresco restaurants rushing inside to finish their meals, quick downpours are often just what's needed to cool things down on hot days, not to mention a great excuse to get out of the sun and shop for souvenirs in the air conditioning.

The weather may be ideal even during the Atlantic hurricane season, which runs from June to October. When it's acting up and a storm is on the way, meteorological authorities like NOAA (National Oceanic and Atmospheric Administration) offer adequate notice to enable plans to be rescheduled. Hurricane season in the Caribbean means fewer visitors to popular locations, however, it's still a good idea to get travel insurance for peace of mind.

Mediterranean: Take a cue from the Italians, who take a full summer month off work to enjoy beaches, coastal trattorias, and strolling up and down the cobblestone roads and yacht-ringed ports of island villages around the Mediterranean.

Summer is the busiest season for Mediterranean cruises, although the season runs from May to November, with fewer passengers at either end. What matters most is that shops are open and that the sun has adequately warmed the crystalline seas that make the affluent and famous are the Mediterranean playing ports so attractive. Swimming on Mykonos' famed beaches, cannoli sampling in Sicily, and admiring the crimson-topped structures in Dubrovnik are all better done with the sun on your shoulders and a refreshing drink at the finish.

Northern Europe: Because many of Northern Europe's most scenic and ancient city centers are built around ports, the winter months bring frigid winds off the sea and into the streets, forcing residents to stay inside. When the landscape and local hospitality thaw in anticipation of a summer filled with pleasant faces and fresh air, the greatest time to embark on a cruise to Northern Europe is when the scenery and local friendliness thaw.

In addition to the longer hours of sunlight that summer brings to northern latitudes, the temperatures are warm enough to leave thick coats at home and instead pack a pair of binoculars and all the sunscreen you'll need for sparkling sunny days and, if you're in the Norwegian Fjords, more waterfalls insight than you ever imagined possible.

In fact, from May to October, Northern Europe and the Baltics actually emerge from their winter hibernation, and outside eating and drinking are nearly required. June cruises to this area are especially beautiful, as the first taste of summer heightens the excitement and festivals bring towns together to celebrate the season's arrival.

The "Taste of Stockholm" food event, the Archipelago Boat Day (with boat parades), Sweden's National Day, and Midsommar, a two-day stretch of traditional dance and eating, are all held in June in Sweden. Estonia, which lies just over the river, is also celebrating. During June's Old Town Days, Tallinn's capital is all about music and parades, as well as its own version of Midsommar celebrations.

Asia: The greatest season to cruise to Southeast Asia is in the fall and winter when humidity levels are lowest and the weather is most conducive to outdoor activities, such as snorkeling off the coast of Ko Samui, Thailand, or kayaking in Ha Long Bay, Vietnam. The typhoon season, which starts in May and brings deadly deluges of rain and wind, is another reason to avoid Asia in the summer.

Rather, go for the drier, colder months of autumn or winter, or, better yet, spring. Budding trees and blossoming flowers adorn the world's most beautiful gardens on a spring cruise to Asia, while seasonal specialty delicacies (such as sakura mochi and treasured strawberry sweets) find their way onto outdoor snacks stalls in Japan.

South America and Antarctica: The optimum time to cruise is between December and March when the weather and events in South America are at their finest. These months are bright yet mild, with large festivities occurring every other week.

On a cruise to South America, Chile and Peru benefit from long summer days, which are great for taking advantage of their major attractions. Opening hours are at their longest and the locations are at their most luxuriant, from beaches to ancient sites to vineyards and national parks. The Antarctica cruise season is brief, lasting just a few months at the peak of the Southern Hemisphere's summer, but it is for good cause.

Ships may sail over the famed Drake Passage—the open ocean between the southernmost point of South America and the northernmost tip of Antarctica—and into the archipelago of the Antarctic Peninsula from December to March. The remainder of the year is dominated by ice floes and bad weather. Visiting Antarctica during the southern summer means more than just the best weather; it's also peak whale migration season in the region, with whale spouts and humpback whale flukes visible in nearly every direction, keeping curious penguins and giant petrels company in the breathtaking natural scenery. Perhaps the only difficulty is adjusting to the 24-hour daylight. When you realize that a 2 a.m. walk on deck can result in a lonely moment observing a nearby elephant seal resting in the stillness of "night," it's tough to decide to go inside, draw the curtains, and miss out on the wonderful sight just outside for at least another many hours.

Galapagos: The purpose of a Galapagos cruise holiday is to see and experience the finest of the destination's diverse species and breathtaking landscape, which can be done at any time of year. The Galapagos Islands' temperatures don't change much; they're normally about 70 to 80 degrees Fahrenheit. Even in the wet season, you'll frequently find bright skies ideal for hiking and photography, ocean conditions that attract more marine creatures, and mating seasons that bring out the best in species like flamingos, sea lions, and blue-footed boobies.

Hawaii:
Oahu, Hawaii - While Hawaii is a fantastic location all year, the months of May and September are particularly noteworthy for Hawaii cruise itineraries. May is "Mele Mai," a month-long Hawaiian music festival celebrated throughout the islands, providing a soundtrack for the conclusion of the winter trade winds, which carry chilly air from the north over the islands.

Though this may result in wet weather in hilly locations such as Oahu's Ko'olau Range and the Big Island's coffee-growing highlands, cool breezes kiss the beaches and towns, keeping you comfortable at all hours. Another season of transpacific crossings occurs in September when cruises often coincide with Honolulu's Aloha Festivals, block parties, and parades, which include traditional dances, music, costumes, crafts, and food.

You may see spinner dolphins off the coast, marine turtles sunbathing on beaches, and seagulls diving for their food if you visit in either month. Because Hawaii's location in the Pacific Ocean makes it one of the world's most distant places, there is plenty of unique and only-seen-here bird, insect, and marine creature species to excite visitors. It's time to schedule the sailings that will take you to your favorite places now that you've learned the finest times of year to visit them.

Chapter-9

What are the advantages of last-minute cruise bookings?

Waiting until the last minute to plan your cruise offers certain benefits for individuals who believe that later is better, particularly if you're flexible regarding cabin location, meal hours, and shore excursions. If your primary holiday aim is to get away from the stresses of daily life for a while and enjoy the opulent facilities available aboard a Celebrity Cruises ship, then booking your cruise trip at the last minute may be the perfect option.

How can I obtain a huge discount on last-minute cruises?

If you're looking for a unique way to spend your vacation, consider taking a cruise. Many people appreciate this sort of activity since it allows passengers on the cruise ship to unwind while sailing around the globe. It may be the most thrilling journey you've ever taken.

This sort of holiday excursion is quite economical when compared to other vacation vacations. On some routes, only 10-14 days of travel will exhaust you.You'll have a hard time packing and unpacking your belongings at whatever port you visit. You'll be concerned about what you consume. Consider the drawbacks.

When you're out on the lake, all you have to do is sit back and relax while they take care of the rest. After you've had a great day, your accommodations and meals will be waiting for you. Additionally, you will be notified about other ports that you may visit. Ports may be found in a variety of nations across the globe.

There are a variety of services available that you will undoubtedly love. You will have a day full of excitement and adventure. You do not, however, need to spend a lot of money on your vacation. Find last-minute cruises to cross your line, even if you have to pay a lot of money on this sort of excursion. Last-minute cruises provide the greatest value for money. Accommodation, food, entertainment, and a variety of other amenities should all be included in your cruise. The cruise ship should also provide you with accommodations, transportation, and a variety of other services, all of which should be accessible at short notice.

You must consider the pleasure you will get. When there is entertainment available, there is no need to hunt for a restaurant or go for a walk. During a cruise trip, you must have everything on board. You must make your cruise the most unforgettable vacation you have ever experienced. What is the greatest way to discover a last-minute deal? Be adaptable. Please keep in mind that these cruise companies are responsible for filling the gaps in your speedboat. To minimize delays in their journeys, they will, of course, provide the sites for a very cheap price.

Last-minute cruise services are the same as those given on full-price voyages. There are also, for the most part, short-term cancellations. In this instance, the cruise ship will try to fill the cabins of people who have canceled their vacation for any reason. They anticipated that the rooms would be filled, so instead of vacating them, they would sell them at a discounted rate. This is the most effective method of filling vacancies. Some suggestions will assist you in getting the finest cruise bargain available. It's worth noting that you may save money on a cruise by buying last-minute discounts during the low season.

This is a great time to travel or visit the places that interest you. In certain places, departure dates may be strange, but great cruise excursions aren't concerned with sporadic departures. If you're searching for a larger last-minute cruise, you can enjoy it even more at reasonable rates. Any discount must be reviewed in advance, for example, two months before the holiday. These special offers go fast, so keep checking with Cruise Information Services. Flexibility in terms of travel dates might also help. You may save more money if you openly allow travel dates to be postponed, say by a few days one way or another.

Cruising necessitates a desire for adventure. Don't be frightened to visit a place you've never heard of before. When you see mysterious locations right in front of your eyes, surprises might come just as readily. You can't say no since now is the best moment to put your money to work in another country. If you want to remain up to date on cruise bargains, you'll need to have access to the internet. You'll be able to make the finest option for your long-awaited cruise experience from there.

A fantastic cruise deal is available at the last minute.

Most individuals are used to making snap judgments. Even though it was not well designed, it offers several advantages that help a large number of people. One of them is to put an end to whatever is upsetting them while avoiding the inconvenience and additional expenditures that a last-minute cruise might bring.

So, even if your vacation date is coming, be prepared to sign up for the excellent cruise bargains accessible online the next time you plan a holiday. It's conceivable that as the holiday approaches, the deals may become more beneficial to you. Of course, you should not pass up these chances.

At first sight, it may seem that the cruise price has been cut, but you will always pay more to join the cruise than you would if you had purchased your tickets in advance. This is all true, however, depending on the last-minute cruise package you choose, there are already last-minute bargains available that are all-inclusive. This means you'll save money on both the trip and the foods you consume.

The cruise package usually covers the whole journey, as well as housing, meals (from breakfast to supper, with some cruises including midnight snacks), and all onboard entertainment. When comparing cruise discounts to regular vacations, the cruise is much superior.

Are you curious as to why? Continue reading:

• Excellent 24 hour service

• Elegant and informal/formal meals

• Swimming pool

• Fitness and well-being options

• Day spas and beauty salons

• First-class entertainment in a variety of bars and theaters

• Mess

• Tax-Free Gift Boxes

Can you think of any other vacation packages that provide all of these amenities in one location? Everything is within walking distance, and the lake and moonlight provide a beautiful backdrop. Only aboard a cruise ship with these amenities, which are accessible with last-minute cruise discounts, will you be able to outperform any other vacation you've ever had.

What's the best way to find the best cruise deals?

Simply be flexible, and keep in mind that there are a variety of reasons why cruise companies use "last minute" terminology. Because they have allotted vacant rooms for discounts and last-minute visitors, cruise ships normally make all rooms available. For those who have paid a large fee, the nature of the services and amenities is identical. Some customers cancel their reservations at the last minute, freeing up additional rooms. It was often employed by the cruise operator for last-minute guests who wanted to join the voyage.

How can I obtain the finest last-minute cruise deals?

You might increase your cruise savings by arranging a last-minute package during the low season, when rates are at their lowest, or you can visit areas that interest you but have irregular departure dates. If you're searching for a last-minute cruise discount, here are some choices.

• Check two months before your trip date and return often, since deals and savings are effective instantly.

• Be flexible: You might save even more money by changing your vacation plans for a few days.

• Be daring: If you find a terrific price on an odd cruise to a place you've never gone, take advantage of it! You will not only save money, but you will also get the opportunity to see a new location. They are usually available at low entry-level costs.

• Use the internet to keep up with the most recent cruise discounts. As cruise companies advertise available vacations, the internet is constantly updated with information about cruise offers.

• It is yet to be decided. Learn all there is to know about the cruise you wish to take. There are many different sorts of cruises available, each with its own set of themes. To guarantee your entire enjoyment, you must carefully choose the sort of cruise.

So don't delay if you're looking for a last-minute cruise holiday. Follow the advice instead, and the enjoyment will be waiting for you on your next trip.

When is the best month to go on a cruise?

Though there are peak cruise booking seasons, the choice to book at a certain or "optimal" time is based on your requirements, goals, and itinerary. The ideal months to book a cruise for next year's summer itinerary are September and October, particularly for Mediterranean cruises and other popular holiday cruises.

Throughout the year, several deals are available. Even though it's not the optimal time to book, you can come across a unique deal that you should take advantage of if it saves you money. If you know you'll be spending time at the spa during your trip, a special offer that allows you to save money on an upgrade to AquaClass is a terrific alternative. If you're a gourmet who wants to sample all of the specialized eateries on board, and you come across a deal that includes a significant onboard credit, take advantage of the discounts and book your cruise.

Cruises on the cheap are a fantastic way to spend your holiday.

Cruises are one of the most popular vacation options available today. A voyage usually lasts three days to three months. A cruise ranges in price from the most affordable to the most costly.

Are there, however, any low-cost cruises? Yes, it is correct. Cruise companies can provide clients with a budget-friendly choice. The cost of an economy cruise often includes lodging, meals, and day and night entertainment. While a low-cost cruise does not always imply bad service or amenities, most cruise companies still assume that all of their passengers are the same. Ascertain that each of your customers has access to the ship's amenities and equipment.

What else is included in the Economy Cruise package?

The following is a typical list of items included in the cost of a budget cruise.

- Air travel, as well as air and sea transfers

- The voyage • The boat's whole enjoyment

- Breakfast, lunch, and supper are all included in the ticket; tea and snacks are also provided at midnight, and room service is available on most voyages.

- Fitness centers, saunas, spas, swimming pools, and other recreational facilities

What will you encounter on your journey?

Both land and water are available for purchase. There are also salons and other beauty facilities to choose from. If you wish to go on a shore excursion, cruise companies provide these to all passengers. In addition, even the most affordable cruisers come with a hydraulic stabilizer, which lowers the boat's movement in harsh weather. This will keep you from passing out or vomiting, and it will keep you comfortable even in strong seas.

Some cruises are susceptible to minor movement in some of the destinations. A cruise ship, on the other hand, is very unlikely to create anything more than minor issues. On a cruise ship, all of these things are commonplace. Of course, if you're talking about a vacation, you should offer some advice and pointers.

Here are some cruise trip suggestions.

1. Like any other cruise ship, economy cruises vary widely in size and construction. For trips that can take 2,500 people overseas or lengthy travels, there is a cruise ship that can carry 100 passengers through tiny waterways.

2. Depending on the price of an economic cruise, you may select between an inside cabin with regular light and a big window and balcony or an outdoor cabin with a huge window and balcony.

3. You must choose a trip that travels to your desired destination. You may take a year-round Caribbean cruise at a reasonable price. In the summer, though, you may take a low-cost Alaska cruise.

4. You may spend the night on the beach by bringing a travel bag. They normally pick up their bags the day before the cruise sails from the ports. However, if you still want to see the ocean at night, you'll need to carry additional clothing and other essentials with you.

5. If you've chosen a cruise that only visits one destination, we suggest bringing your passport for identification purposes.

6. While economy cruises are casual during the day, there may be instances at night when you will need to dress up, so pack or rent formal attire.

7. While onboard entertainment is included in the cost of the budget cruise, day tours and other beach activities may be extra.

8. Don't forget to bring your travel insurance. Low-cost cruise lines are not liable for anything that is lost or destroyed.

9. There are low-cost cruises where you can get a feel for the ships before committing to a vacation. Use it to assess the cruise's overall quality.

You will enjoy a good trip that matches your expectations if you follow these suggestions. Keep in mind, however, that an economy cruise, like any other holiday, should provide you with the best in leisure and comfort. Vacations should also be a source of relaxation rather than tension.

Do cruises get less costly as the departure date approaches?

A last-minute cruise is booked at the end of the booking window, between three and eight weeks before the cruise's departure date, with six to eight weeks being the best range.

The best time to book the last minute is six to eight weeks before the cruise leaves since it is within the timeframe for individuals who bought early to cancel their reservation without penalty. Because someone else has recently opted out, you could be able to get a mid-ship veranda cabin or a top-deck stateroom. To fill such cabins before the sail date, the cruise ticket may reduce during this period.

Find the greatest bargain on last-minute cruises.

They claim that booking cruises in advance might save you a lot of money. Most shipping businesses prefer to pre-book their boats with dependable tourists so they know how many passengers they'll have. On the other hand, you can still get it right if you make your reservation at the last minute.

To be fair, last-minute cruises may also provide significant savings. Last-minute appointments, on the other hand, might be quite dangerous. One danger is that the ship may be completely booked for morning trips, leaving no space for last-minute ticket holders. However, if you live far from the airport or port, aircraft tickets might be quite costly. As quickly as feasible, both the aircraft and the freight businesses enter the booking flow. Low prices are available if you book ahead of time. As a result, a last-minute cruise might be highly expensive. If not done correctly, waiting until the last minute might lead to issues. On a last-minute cruise, you must be cautious.

You must compare all of the cruise lines to obtain the greatest pricing. Several firms provide more convenient departure hours. These are typically last-minute cruises for which there is no other option except to book at the last minute. For example, depending on the number of passengers assigned to each cruise, the firm may raise discounts.

If you're going on a last-minute cruise, it's critical to leave before sundown to avoid missing out on the best deals. You may also hire a middleman. All of your booking chores may be handled by Middleman. Another advantage of using an online cruise booking system is that you may save a lot of money. You may get simple access by using the online reservation system. Furthermore, reserving online may save you time and effort while allowing you to work from the convenience of your own home or workplace.

Another thing to think about is how flexible your cruise arrangements are. You must be aware of your options. You must also be aware of your destination. It takes a lot of effort to get the best rate on a last-minute cruise. Those who assist themselves are aided by fate. However, if you locate the greatest offer, take advantage of it right away. Bright stars may sometimes be found hiding in gloomy clouds, and it's up to you to discover them.

Basic strategies and tips for securing a last-minute cruise:

• Gather all of your travel agency's significant cruise brochures and flyers. Always pay attention to the cruise ship's qualities. On the internet, you may also get information on boats and bridges. You'll get a better understanding of prices, locations, atmosphere, facilities, recreational opportunities, and sorts of lodging this way.

• Write a description of the locations you wish to go to. As much as possible, speak with travel agencies. Travel agencies can provide you with information about the cruise and its specifics. If not, you may always seek guidance and suggestions from your friends. In Alaska, there are several sites to visit and sights to see.

• Determine how long you'll be on the trip. Consult a travel agency. You may also inquire about their cruise plans with them. The most popular cruises usually last between 5 and 18 days. Some firms, on the other hand, provide lengthier cruises with additional sights and activities.

• Make a budget for how much money you want to spend. The sort of cruise you take will be determined by your budget. Cheap, midrange, extra-luxury, and luxury cruises are all likely to fit within your budget.

It is suggested that you compare these kinds to have a better idea of what to anticipate. You can choose which cruises are the most comfortable and fun for your budget by comparing the main sorts of cruises.

• Last-minute cruises need a quick booking process. Speak with a travel agent over the phone to get it perfect. Don't be afraid to notify the agent about your budget and requirements. Aside from that, you might go through several catalogs to discover which cruises would be best for you.

• Use the assistance of a travel agent to find the cheapest departure place. Then make a reservation at the tourist information center for your starting place. Not only that, but you'll have to shell out extra cash for transportation. Don't forget to keep up with the latest cruise data. Ship reviews and other critical information might help you obtain a better deal. It is preferable to plan ahead of time for the cruise.

Some pointers to help you discover the greatest last-minute cruise :

• Before checking for last-minute price decreases, have a few alternate itinerary possibilities in mind. By accident, you could come upon the most interesting cruise possibility.

• Look through the deck layout to make sure you know where your cabin is. Also, keep in mind that suites seldom receive significant price reductions.

• If you live within driving distance of a cruise port, keep an open mind about the ships and itineraries that depart from there.

CHAPTER -10

While you're on a cruise, book a cruise.

When you're on a cruise, one of the finest times to book is when you're already on a cruise. Onboard our ships, we have booking consultants that are glad to meet with you and assist you in planning your next voyage. Whether it's an early mealtime, a comparable cabin position near the pool, or a new place you haven't visited before, our professionals will help you locate precisely what you want to make your next cruise even more unique.

Another advantage of booking your future vacation while aboard is that there are often attractive incentives for doing so. Bonuses vary based on the route and date of your cruise purchase, but you'll often notice special deals such as dollars off or onboard credit for spa services, cocktails, shore excursions, and other activities. You can even be awarded a complimentary drink bundle or a stateroom upgrade.

These exceptional limited-time bargains (you must book before your cruise's final day) are well worth looking into. You'll probably see them promoted on your trip, but if not, stop by the bookings lounge and inquire about any onboard booking deals that are available. Check your daily Today agenda of onboard activities to see if there are any destination-focused information sessions if you're not sure where you want to sail next.

These educational sessions are led by a travel expert who can tell you everything you need to know about cruising to the featured destination, whether it's the Galapagos Islands' magnificent beauty and incredible wildlife, the Mediterranean's cobblestone villages and vibrant cities, or Southeast Asia's exotic and magical cities.

When is the best time to schedule an Alaska cruise?

If you're planning an Alaska cruise, you'll want to book as soon as possible, whether you want to go in the shoulder season (June through August), when there will be fewer tourists and the weather will be dryer, or in the peak season (June through August), when the weather will be hotter. During shoulder season, the first-published fares may be the best available, and Celebrity's Best Price Guarantee assures you'll benefit from any price changes.

If you're going on a cruise to Alaska during peak season, from June to August, you'll want to book early to get the best suites and accommodations. Another reason to book early is to avoid missing out on popular shore activities like glacier helicopter rides.

When is the best time to plan a Caribbean cruise?

When you want to sail, the ideal time to schedule a Caribbean cruise is. The Caribbean's peak season runs from December to April, which includes the popular winter and spring vacations. These Caribbean cruises sell out quickly, so register your cabin or suite, preferred meal times, spa appointments, and specialty dining reservations as soon as possible.

If you're planning a Caribbean cruise in the late summer or early autumn (shoulder season), reserving last minute might save you money, particularly if you have no work or school obligations, are open to different cabin options, and don't mind traveling during hurricane season.

Chapter -11

Taking Care of a Fantastic Opportunity on a Cruise Ship

Almost everyone who works in a precarious position wishes to find a job. They're seeking a job that will allow them to move on to greater pastures. Today's level of life is prohibitively costly. If you have a family to support, your income from a certain company may not be enough to satisfy your daily demands.

You may uncover a range of options if you persist in seeking the proper employment. Being successful takes a great deal of dedication on your behalf. It's also more advantageous if you know how to compare yourself to your peers. With millions of job applicants, you must possess all of the necessary talents and competencies to get hired. You'll encounter several prospects who are vying for your attention.

Rather of instilling anxiety by portraying your competitors as your primary task, make an effort to do harder. This is how life works; you have an edge over them, and they have an advantage over you. You may now change jobs if your current one isn't providing you with what you want monetarily or socially. Change your focus to something new, a vocation that will undoubtedly have a significant influence on your mundane old employment.

Cruise jobs provide a unique experience. You will have the opportunity to work on a variety of amazing cruise ships all around the globe. Take advantage of the chance to have fun while sailing the continents' biggest and deepest waters. You will make money while also enjoying your career since it has the potential to inspire you. By the end of the year, assessments predict that roughly 250 ocean-going cruise ships will be in operation.

Furthermore, according to some studies, approximately 8.5 million Americans go to other regions of the globe each year, particularly during the cruise season. In other words, it provides several options for people interested in working aboard ships. These are possibilities that we must seize.

The more cruise lines you apply to, the more likely you are to be hired. Knowing this, and knowing that you possess the qualities they want, why not apply for one of the cruise companies mentioned? Cruise liners, like crew agencies, do not issue rejection letters. It's a waste of money to apply to a crew agency.

Some things to consider before applying for a cruise ship job:

1. Enquire About Open Vacancies - If you have the chance to read articles or adverts about available positions for ship occupations, you should first inquire about them.

2. Determine if the job is a good fit for your skills. Before the employer can provide you with advice on training and interviews, you must first evaluate your abilities. Have your request executed if you are certain you will be approved.

If, on the other hand, you believe you are failing, you must accept responsibility for your errors. An offer may be made that suits your credentials.

3. Request the specific address for your CV - Now that you've double-checked your credentials, you may send it to the location shown in the classified advertisements.

The following are some of the potential cruise ship jobs:

- Photographers
- Youth advisors
- Chefs
- Restaurant service employees
- Pub technical assistance

You may email your resume straight to the cruise line's address. Although certain shipping companies allow it, mailing your application through a business package is more official and respectful.

Make sure all of your accessories are complete before shipping. Include all of your testimonials and certificates from your previous employers.

A CV, cover letter, at least two reference letters, quotations and accolades, and a picture should all be included in your application.

Best of luck with your new job!

Relax and enjoy your cruise holiday.

Cruising is the most fascinating pastime for adventurers. They would rather spend their time seeing the world's treasures than engaging in tedious pastimes. Every time they go on a cruise, they are pleased; it is a once-in-a-lifetime event for them.

Cruises may be the finest alternative for getting out of town or visiting other regions of the globe. It will enable you to realize your ambition. For visitors, going on a cruise is an exciting experience. It'll make you gasp for air!

Many cruise companies are advertising exclusive amenities for travelers. Because of the many competitors that exist, they must provide the finest onboard comfort to their consumers. Before beginning your cruise trip, there are several variables to consider. The most significant factors to consider are the price, the package, the cruise locations, and a variety of other factors.

When everything is going smoothly, you will always love cruises. Your cruise reservation and timetable must be meticulously arranged. It's a way to skip all the trouble while still enjoying the pleasures of a cruise. The importance of planning for your cruise cannot be overstated. It will assist you in making selections that are in line with your expectations.

The measures to follow to guarantee a pleasant cruise:

1. A package tailored to your requirements: packages differ depending on whether the trip is for an individual or a group. This will also affect how much money you'll have to pay.

You may also ask some questions, which will be answered if the package is for a group. Depending on your interests, most cruise lines offer a variety of discounts. Furthermore, the bundle is dependent on the routes you wish to take.

2. Cruise duration: This must be included in your preparation. It's entirely up to you whether you want to go on a cruise for a few days or a week. You may be able to utilize it for longer periods if you desire more in-depth investigation.

3. Itineraries: Sailing is much more enjoyable when you get to visit some of your favorite destinations on the planet. Make sure you spend your time alone or with your family in the nicest areas possible.

When you get along with your children, you might select cruise locations that they are likely to like, such as somewhere they have never been before. If you've been surfing for a while, on the other hand, you may choose the ones you've never visited before.

4. Cruises: You'll be able to meet the main cruise lines that provide world-class services. The simplest approach to accomplish this is to simply go online and visit the websites that direct you to cruise lines. There are a few factors to look at when choosing a cruise line, including the price if it is reasonable, and the amenities it provides.

5. Doors - Check to see whether the doors are easily accessible so you don't have to pay more to go in. It will also help you save time and effort. Your vacation time will be fulfilled if you plan yourself based on the things stated when shopping. Cruises need meticulous preparation so that you may do anything you want with no regrets after your experience.

You may, for example, visit unique locations by choosing vacation destinations. You don't want your cruises to become a yearly tradition. You should do additional research.

Don't stick to the same strategy all of the time. Remember that one of your cruise objectives is to have an experience, which necessitates a constantly changing atmosphere.

Make your cruise a once-in-a-lifetime event. Always keep in mind that properly organizing your cruise will guarantee that you and your family and friends have an amazing time.

To minimize annoyance, plan your cruise holiday ahead of time

Cruises are one of the most exciting and enjoyable holiday options for you and your family. Many individuals dream of going on a cruise at least once in their lives. This is because cruise companies provide holidaymakers with unique deals. Cruises are like floating hotels that travel across the ocean while providing all of the facilities of a hotel. Casinos, swimming pools, theaters, restaurants, shops or boutiques, spas, gyms, and other amenities are available.

As appealing as a cruise holiday may seem, you should always know how to organize a cruise vacation appropriately. You should be informed of the many sorts of cruise packages available. You must know how to pick a cruise that fulfills your expectations or demands while organizing a cruise holiday. When arranging your cruise holiday, keep the following criteria in mind:

• **Who are you going with?**

There are a variety of cruise packages to choose from. Packages are available for the whole family as well as for single visitors. You're probably thinking about who you'll be bringing on vacation with you. Are you bringing your whole family, including your children? Maybe you're planning a romantic holiday with your lover. There are a variety of cruise packages available to suit everyone's needs.

• **What is the duration of the cruise?**

Cruises usually begin after three nights and run between seven and fourteen days. Determine what is best for you. To enjoy a relaxing vacation, you must first choose how long you want to spend away from home. Perhaps your supervisor has recently given you a brief vacation and you don't want to worry about missing work.

- **What is your favorite trip destination?**

Most individuals have some concept of where they want to go when they decide where to go. It might be a chilly environment like Alaska, or a warmer and more tropical one like the Caribbean or South America. It all depends on your preferences. Many of the well-known cruise companies provide a broad range of popular locations from which passengers may pick. You may contact their offices to inquire about the destinations they provide, or you can visit their website to look at their destination packages.

- **Departure point**

You should think about the cruise ship's departure port. You don't want to spend a lot of money on airline tickets or travel across the nation to get to your cruise departure port. It is important to be aware of the departure port to prevent lengthy flights or costly aircraft tickets.

- **The voyage**

It is important to determine which cruise you plan to take for your holiday. To guarantee optimal comfort and relaxation, you should know what facilities a cruise provides. Onboard, most cruise companies provide a wide range of activities and services. If you like gambling, a casino cruise is generally the best option, and if you're traveling with children, a cruise with kid-friendly activities and amenities is likely the best option. A specific ship caters to couples looking for a romantic trip. If you're planning a honeymoon with your boyfriend or your wife, this yacht is great.

- **Physical activity on the ground**

Going on a cruise doesn't mean you have to spend your whole holiday on the ship.

Land and land excursions are available on several cruise lines. It's usually a good idea to select a cruise that includes guided shore excursions if you want to explore more of the area. On cruise ships, shore excursions are a fantastic opportunity to learn about new cultures and countries. Once a point of contact is established, there are several things to perform.

Kayaking, snorkeling, and even shopping at the stopover markets are all options. Following these recommendations will help you organize your cruise holiday more effectively. Always keep in mind that careful preparation will lead to a more enjoyable cruise trip.

The fundamentals of economic cruises are discussed

Cruises may be both soothing and joyful. A trip to escape the monotony of your life is for you if you want to be wary and fatigued all of the time and life no longer seems to turn you on. Some individuals believe that taking a cruise can only cost a certain amount of money. Fortunately, several cruise companies provide low-cost vacations with excellent activities and cuisine. To take things a step further, this essay delves further into the fundamental components of budget cruises.

What Makes Cruises Truly "Affordable"?
What does a consumer anticipate from a transaction like this, and what does he receive in exchange for his money?

Economy cruises are made up of a variety of components. The following are some of the elements that influence cruise prices.

- **the cost of a cruise**

Some improvements and amenities are included in the cruise fee. Onboard most cheap cruises, there is very little entertainment and amusement. Some cruise lines, on the other hand, provide less expensive services and accommodations, as well as onboard activities.

- **Certain levies for tolls and port duties**

In general, the tariffs and other taxes imposed by various ports have an impact on the cost of inexpensive cruises. When it comes to passenger payments, economy cruises offer a wide variety of rates.

With these rates, some cheap cruises do not cover the passenger fee. Most low-cost cruises, on the other hand, charge passengers parking costs in advance. If there are 20 people on board, for example, the shipping company's authorities will enforce an investigative charging process. The port police personnel get reimbursed for the expense of parking the vessel. The money received will be utilized to keep the port's infrastructure, services, and other operations in good shape.

- **In conclusion, regarding the expense of the flight**

Aerial and marine programs are available on several low-cost cruise lines. This application plots the passenger's route from his or her residence to the port location. Passengers who use this sort of program benefit from extra services in a variety of ways. Cruise lines provide complimentary luggage handling and transportation from the airport to the dock for its passengers. Budget cruises with air and sea programs also assist customers in finding reduced accommodations and meals.

Many low-cost cruises are now available for you to board. The majority of them claim that despite their low prices, they give high-quality service. It's challenging to choose the best affordable cruises. When looking for the finest budget cruises, there are a few factors to keep in mind.

- Just because you're getting a cheap cruise cost doesn't imply you're getting low-quality service. The ship must give more space for suites and rooms for the client. A separate area for the bedroom and living room would be ideal. Several low-cost cruise lines exclusively provide ordinary staterooms with no balconies. Select the cruise ship with the most spacious cabins and bathrooms. To put it another way, it's important to check the ship before embarking.

• Be wary of low-cost cruises that negate the value of insurance. Remember that if the client cancels his insurance, he will not be protected by his services in the case of sickness or injury while navigating.

• Read and study the adverts, brochures, and flyers for low-cost cruises carefully. Some advertisements try to persuade people by providing a lot of information and tasty writing, but this isn't always the case. The true cost should not be concealed.

• Stay away from initial rates. The majority of the low pricing is intended just to capture prospective buyers' attention. Take a look at the costs and lodging options. There can't be any unsightly rooms or cabins on a budget cruise holiday. The award may be given to everyone, not only certain inhabitants of the old.

• Obey the rules set out by the different travel providers. As much as feasible, compare the pricing of various cruise lines. Make cruises in the economy a bit more pleasurable. Make sure to have extra cash in case you run into any unexpected charges. As a rule of thumb, make sure you're secure first. Don't give up if you're content with low-cost cruises. It's a good idea to do some preliminary investigation. So, after everything is in order, pack your luggage and relax while on the cruise.

How to acquire a cruise at a lower price

When you're looking for a unique holiday experience, cruises are one of the alternatives. Modern cruise companies have a variety of amenities that will entice you to stay for a week or two. On a cruise ship, you may enjoy lounges, swimming pools, casinos, gymnasiums, beauty shops, massage parlors, and spas.

If you're afraid about missing out on certain delicacies at home, don't be. These cruises also provide the greatest cuisine, whether Oriental, French, Mediterranean or Italian, to keep your tummy full for the duration of your cruise holiday. After the holidays, you may acquire even more weight! All of this is included in the cruise lines' vacation packages. You can anticipate it to cost well over a thousand dollars due to the many comforts and delectable snacks on board.

You intend to go on a cruise that is within your budget. What's the best way to obtain one?

Before you book your trip, the first thing you need to do is make a detailed strategy.

In such a scenario, you have two choices: employ a travel agency to handle everything for you so you can get the affordable cruise you want, or do it yourself. The second alternative is recommended if you are arranging a cruise within your budget. Instead of paying hundreds of dollars to your travel agency, consider adding the commission to your cruise bill. When planning your cruise, keep these points in mind.

1. Ask for cruise brochures from several travel companies. Check out some cruise deals. It will assist you in selecting the finest trip locations, lodging options, and onboard amenities.

2. Read these brochures once you've acquired them. Consider the places you'd want to visit. Sailing routes to major locations such as the Caribbean, Mexico, and Alaska are available on almost all cruise lines. There's a good chance that these locations will offer a cruise package at a reduced price.

3. Determine the duration of your trip. Cruises should last between three days and two weeks, although some may go up to a month.

4. Consider how much money you'll be spending on your cruise holiday. Cruises are divided into four categories: economy, midrange, luxury, and ultra-luxury. Compare and contrast these categories to see which you can afford.

5. If you are unable to retain your reservation on the day of departure, you may be able to collect cancellation costs. Inquire with your travel agent about cruise line expenses.

When you've made your decision, the following step is to book a cheap cruise. As previously said, cruise packages are divided into four categories: affordable, moderate, luxury, and ultra-luxury. Discounts are available in all of these package types, but not always.

So, when you're ready, here are some recommendations to help you save money on your luxury cruise:

1. Go on a cruise during the off-season. It's not your purpose to boast about vacations; it's to take a vacation. When your budget is low, there is no need to take your vacation during peak season. Prices are rising, just as they are for plane travel.

2. Book a few weeks before or after peak season if you wish to go during the high season. Following this advice can help you save money.

3. Choose a cruise company and a cruise ship that you want to sail on. Examine the cruise lines that provide discounts on your cruise package in the travel brochures you've gathered.

4. Choose an inside cabin if you expect to spend more time in the cabin. It's reasonably priced, however since there is no natural light in the room, you never know what time it is. Get a watch in this casing.

5. Contact your travel agent if you are unable to discover affordable cruise packages on cruise lines. Travel agencies, like air consolidators, may buy tickets in bulk. As a result, they can provide luxury cruises at a lower cost.

Cheap cruises provide a fantastic holiday at a minimal cost

A trip aboard a cruise ship is the epitome of relaxation and romance. Cruises should be on your bucket list if you're planning a trip. It's a fantastic way to spend time with your family or consider it for your honeymoon. Many individuals dream about taking a cruise since it is such a gorgeous and relaxing holiday.

Consider focusing only on relaxing for a week or longer. You will not have the same luxuries and services as if you traveled by air to an exotic place aboard a cruise ship. While planes can get you to your destination quicker, cruise lines provide convenience and a variety of activities.

Enjoy a soothing swim in the cruise ship's pool while taking in the breathtaking views of the sea, or mingle with other guests at the bar. Instead of restricted confines on flights, you may have a magnificent supper in a regal dining room in the evening. Onboard the ship, you may also have a peaceful massage from a therapist. Taking a cruise ship to your holiday destination might make you feel calm and happy than flying.

Many individuals, however, believe that cruising is costly. It is a frequent blunder made by humans. There are cruise packages available to fit practically everyone's needs. If you can afford it, you may upgrade to the more costly package, which includes butlers who will manage your bar from their room, or you can save money by flying economy. They are both the same; you will not be considered as an outcast or an unwanted visitor if you fly economy class.

The employees of cruise ships are very professional and treat guests in economy class as if they were in first class. The main difference is that first-class passengers often have bigger accommodations and butler service. The ship's bar and casino are open to all guests. The ship's amenities, like swimming pools and hot tubs, are open to the public. The cuisine on the cruises is diverse; you may have a lavish supper or just have burgers or hot dogs for lunch. Whatever you're looking for is typically available.

Here are some pointers to keep in mind if you wish to go on a cruise on a budget:

• Consult a travel agency. A skilled travel agent will be able to recommend outstanding cruises that will fit your vacation preferences. He or she can help you locate the ideal cruise for your budget. Tell your travel agent how much money you wish to spend on a cruise and how many others will be joining you. They can almost always get you the greatest discounts, even if your budget is restricted. Make sure you select a cruise and vacation specialist while looking for a travel agency.

• When you book ahead of time, you get a discount. Customers who book in advance get big savings from cruise operators. If you book a month in advance of your cruise, you may save a lot of money. Early booking discounts are offered by cruise lines to fill their ships as soon as possible.

• Booking late also entails significant savings. At some point, a traveler will have to cancel their trip at the last minute. As a result, cruise operators would give significant discounts in exchange for full their ships.

• Inquire about themed bundles. If you're traveling with a group of friends or family, these packages are great. Many cruise companies provide discounts to groups of people. Most cruise companies offer honeymoon discounts, even if you're not on your honeymoon.

• Look for packages on the internet. To learn more about the various cruise packages and their rates, go to the cruise websites. You'll find a wide range of cruise packages here, as well as the ability to compare costs. Some cruise operators also provide discounts for reservations made online.

• If you have previously traveled on cruise lines, we suggest that you sail with the same shipping firm as before. Many cruise companies provide incentives to returning passengers. Here's something to think about. It's not just about the price when it comes to a good bargain; it's also about the overall enjoyment of the trip. This is the real thing when a cruise surpasses your expectations and you return home pleased and satisfied.

A cruise trip is supposed to be enjoyable and relaxing. This is a wasted vacation if you paid for an inexpensive cruise but didn't receive what you anticipated. You must be able to relax and enjoy your trip without thinking about your finances. Take the procedures outlined above to book a low-cost cruise for your holiday.

The top cruises have been chosen

Sailing is a thrilling and enjoyable activity. It's the most cost-effective way to go away. Sailing is a once-in-a-lifetime experience that includes both ocean and land activities. A cruise is arguably the ideal way to spend your honeymoon if you are a newlywed couple. The majority of people perceive cruises to be costly pastimes. Getting a ticket costs thousands of dollars. On the other hand, there are wonderful options for making your cruise fantasy a reality.

The first thing to think about is the cruise itinerary. You may save a lot of money if you plan your trip carefully. This gives you more time to look into the greatest cruise bargains and discounts.

A cruise trip may also be a cost-effective option to see a new cruise location and have a wonderful holiday. However, researching the top cruise lines is also a smart idea. The greatest cruise lines should be able to provide reasonable prices and commissions to their customers. Aside from that, cruise companies must provide excellent customer service.

There are numerous stunning cruise lines to pick from when it comes to cruise lines. Each one offers to transport you to a variety of locations. But that's not all; a long voyage is about much more than simply the destination. The huge range of cruise services offered by cruise companies is one of the nicest things about them. The finest cruise lines, for example, must be able to travel from one location to another.

Alaska, Hawaii, the Mexico Canal, the Panama Canal, and the Caribbean Sea are the most popular cruise destinations. This is where the greatest cruise should take you. Large voyages, on the other hand, should be as inexpensive as feasible. The importance of currency cannot be overstated. However, we must also look after them. Some slogans are just intended to catch your attention.

The finest cruise lines must be both inexpensive and luxurious. You must aim to offer the consumer a taste of an excellent experience without overcharging them. Another key consideration is that cruise companies are required to provide a wide range of facilities and services that are not available on any other sort of trip.

Additionally, customers must get appropriate customer service. Onboard the ship, for example, spa treatments, evening recreational events, dancing classes, sports activities, casinos, entertainment, and a variety of other leisure activities are available. The greatest cruise lines must also exercise extreme caution when it comes to the cuisine they offer. It has to provide both innovative and classic cuisines. It's also important to pay attention to the meal's progression.

If you want to eat, for example, you can eat anything you want, whenever you want. It's advisable to conduct some research to identify the top cruise lines. You'll be able to discover the best deal this way. You may also choose the best sort of cruise line for your requirements and budget.

You can search for the top cruise lines online with confidence. Many websites provide information on the top cruise lines. However, several websites guide how to choose the ideal cruise. Many variables must be included in the ideal boat. It's also beneficial to have a sufficient amount of knowledge. If the room is at the bottom of the ship, for example, the chambers are usually cheap.

The suite, on the other hand, is the most luxurious alternative for the area. Booking as soon as possible is also a good method to narrow down cruise lines. If you book as early as possible, most cruise lines will give you substantial discounts and incentives. The cruise destination should be considered as a reference for selecting the ideal cruise. The port description will almost always be provided by the shipping company.

Always keep in mind that the greatest cruise lines should want to provide you with the best possible service at the best possible pricing. One of the elements used to determine the top cruise lines is the cruise itinerary. Programs should be enjoyable and soothing. You should seek activities such as snorkeling, fishing, diving, viewing movies on board, nightclubs, ballroom dancing, and more.

It is essential to choose the finest cruise lines to make the vacation more peaceful and enjoyable. To take advantage of this fantastic deal, contact the shipping firm as soon as feasible.

Singles Cruises: The Best Place for Singles to Meet Other Singles

Because of the growing demand for cruise ships, the number of individual passengers who want to spend part of their valuable time on a trip is rapidly expanding. During Valentine's season, the number of solo travelers is normally at its highest. Singles Cruises will be providing special pricing for Singles, Singles Activities, and other Valentine's Day activities during this period. Individual cruises are the finest way to round off your one-of-a-kind journey.

Many singles are known to be disappointed on Valentine's Day. Furthermore, the majority of these individuals find it tough to go out every year in pursuit of a Valentine's Day date. It's usually because they're either too timid or don't have enough time to go out on a date. So, for all the singles who are on the verge of giving up seeking a date, it would be better if they saved up all of their money and joined Singles Cruises.

You're a stranger to everyone on the Singles Cruise while you're on your own. As a consequence, even while surrounded by strangers, those who know what Singles Cruise is for frequently feel more at ease and calm. This allows you to meet new people and feel more adaptable and at ease in their company. Who knows, your future mate may be just around the corner or right in front of you while you're busy meeting new acquaintances. The many activities that various cruises offer their passengers ensure this.

Individual cruising is already well-known as a cost-effective method to meet new people, and many singles choose to cruise alone since it provides them with unique and interesting opportunities, closeness, and experiences with others. who are capable of becoming friends, or at the very least excellent friends...

A single Caribbean cruise is a terrific alternative for you if you want to enjoy the blazing sun, lovely resorts, and a limited rum punch. A Unique European Cruise, on the other hand, is ideal for hopeless romantics who wish to drink a glass of red wine beneath the full moon. Whatever your preferences, there will always be a Singles Cruise to fit you. All you have to do now is figure out which cruise company offers the finest singles bargains and which cruise line best suits your likes and preferences.

Here are some thorough guidelines to assist you in making your decision:

1. A one-time fee is charged to solo passengers. Because most cabins are built for two people, most cruises only allow one extra guest per room at an additional expense. You don't expect to spend an additional 150-200 percent, but you do expect it to be costly.

2. On certain voyages, the supplement is waived during promotions, but you are assigned to a room with another passenger. If you don't want your privacy invaded or if you don't want to share a room with another person, a single room supplement is a decent option. You can still take advantage of the offer if you're the sort of person who considers being in a room with someone the most engaging.

3. Look through the brochure or search the internet to see if any cruises are still available. In certain cases, a cruise has been pre-booked by a singles group that only enables its members to participate. However, most of these organizations enable non-members to contact them as well, although at a higher cost than members. Even though you may join these groups, you will continue to travel alone. Joining them has the benefit of allowing you to meet other singles. If you join a group like this, there is no reason to be hesitant since they are just like you: lone travelers in quest of company and love.

Chapter -12

The Best Ways to Get Ready for Your First Cruise

You're probably wondering how to prepare for a cruise whether you're a first-time cruiser or haven't cruised in a while. Cruise holidays are different from land trips in that they need much less planning. You won't have to seek the finest restaurants to dine at, find trustworthy tour operators, or come up with methods to keep the group entertained—it'll all be done for you aboard the ship.

These suggestions can help you prepare for your first cruise.

This article includes the following sections:

Ensure that all of your travel documents are in order: Even though a passport isn't necessary for the ports you'll visit, it's usually a good idea to cruise with one if you're going to an overseas location. If you need to arrange an unexpected ticket home during your cruise, having a passport will make it much simpler. Make sure your passport isn't expired and that it will be valid for at least six months after your cruise is over. Check the visa requirements for each nation you'll visit to ensure you'll be able to enter.

Obtain local currency by contacting banks: To prevent debit or credit card freezes, notify your bank that you will be going to a different state or country before your cruise. Many banks provide an online system where you may enter your trip dates, or you can phone the customer support number for each card/account you'll be using while away. Obtaining local cash for each of the countries you visit (if they do not take your own country's currency) should also be on your pre-cruise to-do list. You won't have to waste time seeking ATMs or money exchange businesses at the port.

Prepare a packing list: One of the best things about a cruise is that you just have to unpack once since your transportation and accommodations are included. There's no need to overpack because of the onboard laundry service. Regardless of your location, bring a swimsuit to enjoy the swimming and soaking options available onboard in the pools and hot tubs.

T-shirts, swimsuits, and other pool attire are not permitted at any time in the main or specialty restaurants, while shorts and flip-flops are not permitted in the evening. Jeans are acceptable for any occasion as long as they are free of rips and tears. On most evenings, the dress code on Celebrity Cruises is smart casual, which for males includes khakis or jeans and a sports shirt, and for ladies, casual dresses or slacks (including denim) or skirts and blouses.

You may dress up anyway you like on Evening Chic night. Men can wear pants or designer jeans with a dress shirt, button-down shirt, or sweater; a sports coat or blazer is optional. Women can wear a cocktail dress or skirt, pants, or designer jeans with an elegant top, while men can wear pants or designer jeans with a dress shirt, button-down shirt, or sweater.

It's OK if you prefer more formal wear, but it's not required. So leave your tuxedos and evening gowns at home—or don't! Don't stress about remembering which night is which. Celebrity Today, the daily newsletter, which is delivered to your cabin and accessible at the Guest Relations Desk, will serve as your reference to appropriate evening wear.

Hairdryers, curling irons, candles, or open flames of any type, and garment irons are among the objects that are forbidden aboard. If you're concerned about wrinkled clothes, carry a wrinkle spray or leave your outfit in your stateroom's bathroom while you take a shower; the steam will assist to remove creases. Otherwise, avoid carrying wrinkle-prone textiles.

Plan Your Excursions & Adventures Now: There's nothing quite like the excitement of planning a trip. Why not add to the thrill by doing some pre-cruise study on your destinations? Explore our port guides, which include essential information about each port, such as the best places to visit, activities to do, restaurant/cuisine suggestions, transportation options, local culture and history, shopping, and currency and tipping conventions.

While you're at it, have a look at the beach adventures available and add a few to your agenda. Shore excursions provide a fantastic opportunity to enjoy the finest of each port of call, from personalized, luxury experiences to fitness- or family-focused outings.

Tours of historic places are available, as well as experiences on catamarans, boats, and kayaks. You may tailor your holiday activities to your specific interests, from farmers' market excursions for foodies who want to live like a local to hop-on, hop-off buses for tourists who want to see it all.

Learn About Your Ship: If this is your first cruise, you may tour the ship from the comfort of your own home using our website, which includes complete deck plans for each ship in our fleet. You'll find plenty of entertainment, clubs, lounges, and fine dining restaurants to choose from. Whether you're watching a live concert, marveling at a performer as they twist and flip at Eden on Celebrity Edge, or eating al fresco at the Lawn Club Grill, the spaces onboard were created with you in mind.

On sea days, depending on the ship you'll be sailing on, you may practice your basketball, ping-pong, or golf-putting talents, enjoy a friendly game of croquet or bocce at the Lawn Club, or play pool volleyball with the ship's officers.

Make Reservations at Specialty Restaurants: You'll be able to pick from a variety of free and specialized onboard food choices while aboard. However, if you want to dine at one of the best specialty restaurants, you'll need to make a reservation before you set sail. Tastes of the Mediterranean are served in venues inspired by France, Italy, and Greece, while creativity reigns supreme at immersive food experiences like Le Petit Chef, which is the ideal participatory activity for families and groups. Sushi on Five and The Porch Restaurant, for example, provide the finest catches and raw bars at sea for fish aficionados.

Make a Spa Appointment in Your Calendar: Massages, cosmetic treatments, and wellness consultations at The Spa sell up fast, so make your appointment as soon as possible after booking your cruise. Full body wraps, manicures and pedicures, salon treatments, and more are all available, but if you wait until the last minute to schedule your pampering, your selections will be restricted.

Medication should be kept on hand: Make sure you have enough prescription and over-the-counter drugs to last the duration of your vacation. Although every ship has a medical facility, there is no assurance that the drug you need will be accessible. It's always better to be safe than sorry. Also, don't forget to bring sunscreen if you're sailing to a hot location. Lip balm with SPF is especially useful for sunny travels.

For Embarkation Day, bring a day bag: You'll be separated from your main baggage on embarkation day—it'll be delivered right to your room—so bringing a small bag with a few necessities is a good idea. With Cruises Open Access, you'll have access to your stateroom as soon as you board, so you won't have to worry about overpacking and carrying your carry-on about until your room is ready.

A few products, such as deodorant or scent, for a refresh, a wardrobe change if you want to go to the pool after getting situated, or a bag with activities to keep the kids engaged may all fit in your carry-on. Whatever you'd bring on an airline as a personal item is okay for your day bag.

Collect all electronic devices and chargers: You'll need to keep your gadgets charged, whether it's your phone, tablet, camera, or eReader (or all of the above!), so be sure to bring your chargers. You may wish to carry an adaptor with you to charge your phone when you go ashore, depending on your location and power demands. Include a daypack or small bag in your luggage for carrying goods like your camera, a water bottle, and sunscreen about the ship or in port.

Online Check-In: Up to 24 hours before your cruise, you may check-in online or through the app. Checking in online speeds up the boarding procedure, allowing you to get started on your holiday sooner. There's no one way to start your first day on a luxury cruise ship: explore the ship, unpack your bags, or relax by the pool. Browse cruise itineraries on the internet now that you know how to plan for a trip.

Chapter -13

The Only Cruise Packing List You'll Ever Need

There's just one thing left to do now before you set sail into the sunset: pack your belongings. Given all of the particular considerations—temperature differences between ports of call, onboard dress standards to follow, and various sorts of shipboard activities and shore excursions to sign up for—packing for a cruise might seem onerous.

And, of course, there's the matter of the destination. A cruise packing list for an active, outdoorsy cruise to Alaska will vary significantly from one for a relaxing beach vacation in the Caribbean or a sophisticated city-hopper cruise in the Mediterranean. Don't worry: an expert-compiled cruise packing list will ensure that you're the savviest sailor on board—and the best-dressed, too. After all, you'd rather spend your valuable time in port shopping for magnificent gifts than scrounging for forgotten knickknacks.

Remember that the benefit of a cruise holiday is that you only have to unpack once after boarding the ship after you've packed everything into your luggage. So browse through this exhaustive list of items to pack for a cruise and you'll be ready to go in no time.

What should I take on a cruise in terms of clothes, shoes, and accessories?

A cruise trip covers a lot of terrains, so you'll need a lot of clothing versatility as well. On the ship, you should be able to easily transition from daytime casual to evening chic, and you should also be able to shift from a fun-in-the-sun beach jaunt to a rainy-day city walking tour.

In the days preceding up to your vacation, keep an eye on the weather predictions and think in terms of layers and mix-and-match combinations to avoid your bag bursting at the seams. Don't be frightened to reuse your more softly used outfits: your fellow cruisers will have no idea if you're wearing the same outfit again.

Attire(Casual):

You'll want a nice assortment of comfy and casual attire for days spent roaming about the ship or port. Check the weather forecast and prepare a cruise packing list that includes a variety of shorts, jeans/khakis, sundresses/skirts, T-shirts (long and short-sleeved), and tank tops.

Dress Code (Formal):

The evenings onboard the ship take on a dressier air, so check the cruise line's dress code to be sure you're on board with the anticipated style. Men should wear a dress or button-down shirts, sweaters, and trousers (even designer jeans) with an optional blazer on Celebrity's refined Evening Chic nights, while women should wear cocktail dresses, a skirt/blouse combination, or a professional pantsuit (nice jeans with an elegant top will do).

If you want to go all out with tuxedos and evening dresses, go for it— after all, it's your vacation. Evening Chic is two evenings on Celebrity cruises of seven nights or longer, and one night on shorter itineraries. On all other days, sophisticated casual dress is permitted in the evenings.

Outerwear:

Check the weather forecast and make sure you've dressed appropriately for the weather. For example, if you're going on an Alaska cruise, you'll almost likely need a lot of layers, as well as waterproof apparel, winter hats, and gloves. A sweater or sweatshirt may be required on a Caribbean cruise, and the same is true for a spring or autumn walk around a Mediterranean port. For bright days on the deck or in port, don't forget sun hats and baseball caps, while ladies may welcome a fancy scarf or shawl to throw over their shoulders for classy nights aboard the ship.

Activewear & Beachwear:

Whether you're splashing about on the pool deck or at the beach, you'll want to carry at least two swimsuits with you so they can dry in between usage. On sun-kissed days, cover-ups provide further protection as well as a seamless transition from swimming to getting a bite to eat. Keep in mind that ships have gyms and outdoor tracks, fitness programs abound, and many ports encourage runners, kayakers, cyclists, and other athletic types—no there's a need to miss your workout if you don't want to, so carry your sportswear with you.

Sleepwear:

After a long day of visiting the port, you'll want to snuggle up in some warm pajamas. Pack comfortable walking shoes, whether sneakers or comfortable flats, for extended trips in port. Dress shoes are required for pricier evening meals onboard, while sandals and flip-flops are required for a pool and beach days. Bring suitable gear, such as rain boots, water shoes, or hiking boots, if the weather is expected to be extremely wet, the beaches are rough, or there are mountains you want to climb.

Accessories

Don't forget about the garnishes! Bring some jewelry if you like, but keep in mind that you'll want to leave your nicest items at home on any vacation. Though cabins include safes, it's best not to show off costly jewelry when in port. Belts and ties may help men complete their ensembles.

A wristwatch is essential, particularly when traveling between time zones (so you don't miss the boat while on an expedition), and an umbrella or poncho may rescue the day if it rains. Eyeglasses and sunglasses should be at the top of your cruise packing list. Bring some protective cases with you as well to assist keep your valuables safe throughout your trip.

Bags:

After you've unloaded your baggage, you'll want to have some smaller bags on hand for the various experiences that await you throughout your cruise. While in port, a daypack and/or beach bag are useful for carrying things. Ladies might consider carrying two purses: one casual handbag for daily outings and another evening handbag for dressier situations.

Adding a foldable bag to your cruise packing list is a smart way to transport any additional items you may pick up along the route. A few plastic bags (for waste and storage), ziplock bags (for waterproof storage and organizing), and a damp bag are all useful additions (for trips to the beach).

Laundry:

Bring a wash bag to store dirty clothes, and consider doing some laundry mid-trip rather than overpacking if you're going on a longer cruise. Laundry services are available on ships, which can help you prevent overpacking.

What hygiene items should I bring on a cruise?

Aside from clothes, shoes, and accessories, you'll want to pack your stateroom bathroom and vanity with all of your favorite personal hygiene goods from home.

Toiletries: While your cabin will be equipped with high-end bath amenities, you may wish to bring along travel-sized bottles of your favorite items. A face cleanser, moisturizer, deodorant, shaving tools, lip balm, Q-tips, and cotton balls/pads are among the other cruise packing list essentials. Also, remember to bring a toothbrush, toothpaste, dental floss, and mouthwash. Contact lens users should bring all necessary equipment (including a case and solution), as well as a pair of tweezers and a nail file, and/or clippers.

Cosmetics for hair and make-up : When you come in after a day at the beach or a windy sea day up on deck, your hair may need a little additional taming. Make sure you have all of the necessary hairstyling supplies, accessories, and equipment, as well as a brush and comb (note that hairdryers are provided in each stateroom). Bring your makeup (and don't forget the remover) with you. You may also want to bring a tiny bottle of perfume or cologne with you to spray.

Products for Health and Safety : Carry any necessary prescriptions (including seasickness treatments, if necessary), pain relievers, vitamins, feminine hygiene products, birth control, and a basic, individualized first-aid kit with you. Sunscreen (and aloe vera for relief, just in case you miss a place), as well as bug protection if you're traveling somewhere tropical, are other items to bring on a cruise. To help keep germs at bay when on the run, have hand wipes and sanitizer close at hand.

What papers should I bring on a cruise?

You're indeed on vacation, but that doesn't imply you can survive just on sunlight and fizzy cocktails. To guarantee that everything goes well, you'll need certain important documents and a well-stocked wallet.

Wallet and Money Belt Accessories

During your travel, you may wish to swap your wallet for a money belt. Bring cash (including small amounts for tips), an ATM or debit card, and credit cards, regardless of which method you use.

Put your driver's license (as well as an international driver's license if you intend on renting a vehicle in another country) in a safe place. Foreign travel also requires the possession of a passport that has been stamped with any relevant visas. You should also have your medical insurance card with you at all times, as well as any travel insurance details.

Contact Information & Documentation

Bring important trip papers with you, such as airline tickets, hotel information, and maps and instructions. The cruise operator will also provide you with baggage tags, which you should attach to your bags before boarding the ship.

Make backup copies of important documents and information in case anything is lost or stolen during your journey. Separate photocopies from originals, and consider having scanned copies kept digitally as well. Important phone numbers (such as credit card companies or emergency contacts back home) should also be accessible, as well as the postal and email addresses of any friends or family you may wish to write to while you're gone.

Should any medical issues emerge, it's also a good idea to preserve copies of any prescriptions you take, as well as a list of drugs and your medical history. A pen and diary will enable you to scribble down anything that may come up on the trip—or to preserve your vacation experiences for posterity—while travel guides will help you to read up on the ports that await you.

What technological things should I bring on a cruise?

All of our favorite technological devices might fill luggage on their own these days! Keep your mobile phone and laptop (or tablet) towards the top of your cruise packing list if you want to be amused digitally and keep up with emails and news from home.

To snap photographs, listen to music, and set an alarm clock in the morning, your mobile phone may be all you need. If that isn't the case, you should carry a good camera (with lenses, memory cards, and so on), music (and a player), and a travel alarm clock with you. All of those devices will need charging, so don't forget to bring your chargers. A power strip (ideally with built-in USB ports) may assist guarantee that there is enough power in the cabin.

Consider using a waterproof phone cover to safeguard your phone if you'll be spending a lot of time by the pool or at the beach. If you're staying in a hotel before or after your cruise, don't forget to bring voltage converters. Finally, if you're going someplace with a lot of animals, like Alaska, a decent set of binoculars will definitely add to the wow factor.

What else should I bring on a cruise?

There are a few additional tidbits to assist you to make your cruise packing list go smoothly.

It's a good idea to bring your favorite snacks, chewing gum, and a reusable water bottle with you on the plane or at the port to keep you fed and hydrated. Long flights or automobile journeys may be made more comfortable with the use of travel aids such as earplugs, a travel cushion, and a sleeping mask. It's always a good idea to have a pack of travel-sized antibacterial wipes on hand to clean down germ-prone surfaces as required.

Whether you like to print, e-books, or magazines, carry some reading materials with you for relaxed hours on your balcony or by the pool. If you're going someplace with a lot of time to spend in the sand and surf, you may want to pack your own snorkel and goggles so you can go snorkeling whenever you want.

If you're traveling with children, you'll need to think of diapers, strollers, toys, and games, among other things. Finally, remember to stow your home and vehicle keys away someplace safe—you won't need them until the end of your vacation, but you'll want to be able to locate them quickly when it's time to go.

Checklist for Packing for a Cruise

Check out our helpful cruise packing checklist to make sure you have everything you need for your trip. Please keep in mind that some of these things may be optional, depending on your cruise location, length, weather, and the sorts of activities you pick.

T-shirts/tank tops

- Sundresses/skirts
- Shorts
- Jeans/khakis
- T-shirts/tank tops

Slacks

- Cocktail dresses/gowns
- Skirts/blouses
- Dressy pantsuits
- Dress shirts
- Blazers/suits/tuxedos
- Slacks
- Cocktail dresses/gowns
- Skirts/blouses
- Sweaters/sweatshirts
- Coats/jackets/raincoats
- Hats/sun hats
- Gloves
- Scarves/shawls

- Outerwear
- Swimsuits
- Cover-ups
- Workout clothes/activewear
- Pajamas
- Beachwear & Activewear
- Sneakers
- Sandals/flip-flops
- Casual shoes
- Dress shoes
- Specialty footwear (hike boots, rainboots, and water shoes)

Accessories

- Belts
- Ties
- Jewelry
- Eyeglasses
- Sunglasses
- Glasses Cases

- Wristwatches
- Umbrella/poncho Bags
- Purses
- Daypacks/beach bags
- Collapsible totes
- Plastic bags

- Ziplock bags
- Wet bags

Laundry kit (detergent/wrinkle-release spray/stain remover)

- Laundry bag
- Toothbrush
- Toothpaste
- Dental floss
- Mouthwash
- Shampoo/conditioner
- Facial cleanser / skincare products
- Moisturizer
- Deodorant
- Lip balm
- Razor
- Shaving cream
- Contact lenses/case/solution/eye drops

Cosmetics for hair and make-up

- Makeup
- Makeup Remover
- Perfume/cologne
- Brush/comb
- Hairstyling equipment
- Hairstyling supplies
- Hair accessories

Products for Health and Safety

- Sunscreen/aloe vera
- Insect repellent
- Hygiene items for women
- Contraception

- Pain relievers
- Medications and vitamins
- First-aid kit
- Medications for seasickness
- Tissues
- Hand sanitizer

Wallet and Money Belt Accessories

- Money belt/wallet containing cash, ATM card, and credit cards
- A valid driver's license or an international driver's license is required.

Passports/visas

- Medical insurance card
- Information about travel insurance

Contact Information & Documentation

- Printed/personal baggage tags
- Maps and instructions
- Travel papers (cruise boarding passes/airline tickets/hotel information/itinerary/etc.)

Travel books and guides

- Prescriptions, medication list, and medical history
- Copies of your passport, essential papers, credit cards, and so forth.
- Addresses/e-mail addresses for friends/relatives
- Small notebook/journal
- Pens/highlighters
- Important phone numbers (credit cards/emergency contacts/etc.)

Technology

- Camera/lenses/memory cards/batteries/charger
- Voltage adapters (for foreign pre-/post-cruise hotels)
- Alarm clock
- Power strip
- Music and player
- Headphones
- Binoculars
- Waterproof phone case
- House/car keys
- Snacks/chewing gum
- Reusable water bottle
- Travel aids (earplugs/sleeping mask/travel pillow)
- Pleasure reading (magazines/books/e-book with charger)
- Antibacterial wipes
- Snorkel/goggles

Now that you know how to pack like an expert, all you need is your cruise ticket and you'll be ready to travel! Explore the itineraries of our 14 advanced ships, which travel to over 300 places throughout the globe. To book your perfect cruise, just go to our website.

Chapter -14

Add These 13 Eco-Friendly Shore Excursions to Your Bucket List

While on a cruise, schedule a sustainable shore excursion to see some of the world's most spectacular natural treasures. There is no lack of magnificent experiences, amazing vistas, and ecologically responsible activities to discover throughout your holiday with over 300 places on itineraries.

Here are thirteen sustainable shore activities to consider on your cruise, ranging from whale viewing to magnificent hikes in picturesque mountain ranges.

This article includes the following sections:

1: Take a stroll around Ephesus' ruins: Explore the adjacent remains of Ephesus, a historic Greco-Roman archeological site, during a stay in Kusadasi. Even though Ephesus was just discovered 150 years ago, parts of its buildings are thought to date back to the seventh century B.C. Take a stroll around this gorgeous UNESCO World Heritage Site and marvel at structures that have survived thousands of years, such as the Library of Celsus and the Temple of Artemis, one of the Seven Wonders of the Ancient World. Fuel up with an organic farm-to-table meal with amazing local tastes and ingredients after a hard day in the sun.

2: Hike in the Balearic Islands: Hike through a local farm in the Sierra de Tramuntana highlands to take in the sun-drenched vistas of Mallorca. Admire the majestic mountain, which stretches for 55 kilometers and is filled with charming towns and tall olive trees. Finish your tour at a lovely vineyard, where you may relax while drinking Spanish wines and nibbling on crudités.

3: Glaciers in Alaska are awe-inspiring: While in Alaska, there is no lack of natural beauty to be discovered. During a stay in Juneau, take a guided tour of the forest around Mendenhall Glacier, one of North America's most accessible glaciers. Admire the glacier's ice blue splendor before heading out on one of the area's numerous hiking paths, where you'll find salmon streams, tumbling waterfalls, and, if you're fortunate, wildlife like black bears, beavers, and bald eagles in their native environment.

4: Visit Ston for Mussel Fishing: During a boat cruise in Ston, just outside of Dubrovnik, savor fresh fish. Ston is recognized as Croatia's oyster capital, and with good reason: the area's oyster beds produce some of the world's most delectable oysters and mussels. Board a rustic boat and set sail towards the region's famed oyster and mussel beds, where you may taste some of the catch. Continue to savor Croatian delights with a decadent supper with regional favorites like black risotto and freshly baked bread.

5: Take in the scenery of Slovenia's coastline: During a guided tour of the area, discover the splendor of Koper's nature and stunning vistas. Take a look around the picturesque town of Izola and its beautiful shoreline. In Iran, admire the Venetian architecture. Also, take a stroll through the distinctive salt farms and fruit plantations near Padna.

6: Go to a Zakynthian Organic Farm: On the island of Zakynthos, visit an organic farm to see the marvels of the Greek countryside. You'll walk through olive oil trees at Theranos Farm and hear about how this family-owned enterprise collects various fruits, vegetables, herbs, and flowers on the island. You'll be able to experience these organic treats, which are an integral element of Greek cuisine, during your tour.

7: Take a whale-watching tour in Juneau: On a whale-watching trip in Alaska's seas, bring your finest camera and a set of binoculars. Keep a lookout for humpback whales, orcas, and seals in the distance, and enjoy seeing these amazing animals break the water.

Outside of Vigo, board a Mussel Farming Boat: In Combarro, a picturesque town just outside of Vigo, go mussel farming. Begin your day excursion by visiting this picturesque hamlet and witnessing the floating docks and elevated stones used for mussel farming and grain drying. Then, on board a beautiful catamaran and sailing out along the Galician coast, you'll learn how mussels are captured in the ocean and enjoy freshly cooked mussels produced from one of the world's most recognized places, you'll get a personal look at mussel farming.

9: Visit the Camargue to see the birds: Discover the marshes of Camargue, a little island near Marseille with a diverse range of vegetation and animals. Take a ride in an all-terrain Jeep through the Camargue's beautiful countryside, where you'll see pink flamingos, herons, and white horses. You may even embark on a horseback ride through the area's salt marshes if you're feeling brave.

10: Go to Rhodes and see a Bee Colony: Visit the famed Bee Museum on the island of Rhodes, where you can discover more about these fascinating animals and their crucial role in nature. Observe bee colonies via glass beehives, which allow you to see their daily activities and social order. Learn about the process of honey extraction and sample some of the island's honey.

In Katakolon, you may learn all there is to know about olive trees:

During your break at Katakolon, Greece, you'll tour through ancient remains and historic monuments to learn about the riches of Ancient Olympia.

Then spend an afternoon visiting a family-run olive farm, where you'll learn about the region's distinctive topography and microclimate, as well as how this makes it ideal for growing a range of olive and grape varieties, including Kalamata, Koroneiki, and raisins.

12: Visit Ketchikan to learn about Native Alaskan history: In Ketchikan, see an actual Native Alaskan hamlet, where you'll be greeted with a traditional dance ritual. Learn about tribal history and listen to locals recount tales about their forefathers and mothers. Then stroll around Ketchikan's totem pole collection, which depicts the history and culture of these people via exquisite carvings.

13: In Aruba, Surround Yourself with Butterflies: The Butterfly Farm and Natural Bridge, two of Aruba's most famous natural attractions, showcase the island's splendor. Stroll through a tranquil tropical garden, where you'll be surrounded by vibrant butterfly species and see a new butterfly emerge from its cocoon.

Alternatively, see the Natural Bridge, a sequence of limestone structures formed overages by ocean water and severe winds. This beautiful rocky environment is the perfect backdrop for a holiday snapshot to remember your time in Aruba.

Chapter -15

Take a break and enjoy Alaska Cruise's thrills and excitement

People nowadays are worried about their own goals. You want to stay up with the fast-paced lifestyle of today's world. They are often exhausted at the end of the day. You don't need to set aside time to unwind. They even forsake sleep until their bodies succumb to dizziness and cramping.

They often skip meals or eat quickly. To keep you going, you have an alarm clock, an appointment calendar, or a planning notebook. Don't you realize that trying to keep up with the frantic pace of modern life might put you in the hospital, or worse, in the grave? Mental and physical exhaustion accumulated over time, but it was neglected, and it may make you ill.

Expect the unexpected! Working, working, working. Isn't it a little excessive?
Why don't you take a breather?

Life should not be lived at a breakneck speed. After all, frequent escapes entrenched in the rigors of your chosen work or industry are the finest way to appreciate life. In your leisure time, you may engage in a variety of soothing activities. Alaska may be the greatest alternative for you if you want to make it more adventurous and entertaining. It's just a question of being excited and perceiving the world's marvels at the same time. There are three main types of Alaska cruise packages available. Each of the packages will provide you with a uniquely Alaskan experience. The following are some of them:

• Interior Alaska Cruise - Take advantage of the chance to see all of Alaska's interior marvels. Icebergs and glaciers will undoubtedly captivate you.

• Alaska Day Cruise - Get a birds-eye perspective of the whole state. You will be visited on a day cruise, as indicated by the package's name. In Alaska, it might have a massive ice wall on the top face.

• Alaska Celebrity Cruise: The Alaska Celebrity Cruise is referred to as the First Class Alaska Cruise. The Celebrity Cruise will also provide you with a more spectacular trip. It is, nevertheless, the most costly of all Alaska cruises.

Humpback whales, fjords, and glaciers are all popular Alaska cruise features. Depending on the bundle you've chosen, you'll be able to view them. Furthermore, nothing compares to the enchantment of Alaska cruises. This is the only site where the ice and animal secrets may be discovered. You may also choose to continue sailing on the ice.

The duration of your stay in Alaska will be determined by the package you choose. The majority of cruises are seven days long. If you plan, you'll have plenty of time to see all of Alaska's cruise destinations. The duration of your stay may be extended up to 14 days or a two-week cruise. You have the option of selecting the boat size that best meets your needs. Sailing on smaller boats with fewer people is sometimes preferable. You can get a better look at the scene.

Unlike the bigger ships with almost a thousand people, it is more difficult to get out of the throng, get a closer look, and even touch the glaciers on the smaller ships. The larger ships also feature more opulent facilities. Smaller ships might astonish you with their unrivaled speed...

You have the option of selecting the most suitable bundle. Choose the best package for your requirements. As a result, Alaska Cruise provides fantastic helicopter flights to the glaciers. You may also take a stroll on the glaciers if you wish to embark on an adventure. You'll never be able to compare your experience to that of an Alaska cruise. Unlike past cruises you've taken when you simply regret how much money you spent, Alaska will be all about joy for you.

The fundamentals of an Alaska cruise

Alaska, sometimes known as the "Ice World," is a state in the United States. With mountains of glaciers and icebergs, Alaska is a wonderfully unique and magnificent region. It's also a location where whales and bears live and prosper, as well as a place with spectacular views of Mother Nature's splendor. It's also a one-of-a-kind cruise destination that combines naturalist and urban elements.

Many cruise ships that have visited the wonders of Alaska can attest to how much they enjoyed their time there. Its heights are overlooked by the mountains. It's fascinating to watch the many animal types in Alaska. These are creatures that are seldom seen in the wild.

The mysterious hue of the Alaskan border is due to a big gathering of grass. Many people think of Alaska as a region blanketed in ice and snow, so these plants are a pleasant surprise. The glittering ice creation may be seen from the coast. Deepwater runs easily, and the color changes to blue as a consequence. The brilliant light reflects the blue sky. The wildflower and herb meadows are stunning.

Sailing Alaska's coastal locations may provide vistas that are not available in any other way. During the voyage, you will be able to see the massive collection of glaciers that meet the ocean in action. Aside from that, the trip may also watch the various lives of Alaskans.

Furthermore, kids will get the chance to see several whale species as they play in their natural environment. Most Alaskan cruises include many interior excursions. The holiday cruise may visit national parks and enjoy nature's intrinsic beauty as a result of this sort of travel.

A cruise to Alaska may provide a terrific vacation with lovely and comfy facilities. Passengers will not only cruise within the ship but will also have the option to take spectacular excursions into the wilderness of mainland Alaska. The cruise ship will automatically dock at a location known as "Tourist City." It is a location where people are disembarked from ships. It is a tiny town with a population of 600 or more people. So, what exactly are you waiting for? Leave your problems at home and go on an Alaska cruise!

With Caribbean cruises, you may discover the magnificence

Consider taking a trip around the globe. You enjoy the beautiful scenery and good weather. The whole world is a paradise...

Thousands, if not millions, of natural marvels, have been bestowed to humanity. Every nation in the world may be proud of its natural resources. The surrounding land and water resources may be seen from the top to the bottom of the global map. The Crusaders had a tough time deciding which location to visit since there are so many options. I'm looking forward to a luxurious trip with Caribbean Cruises.

Consider taking a trip around the globe. You enjoy the beautiful scenery and good weather. The whole world is a paradise... Thousands, if not millions, of natural marvels, have been bestowed to humanity. Every nation in the globe may be proud of its achievements.

The surrounding land and water resources may be seen from the top to the bottom of the global map. The Crusaders had a tough time deciding which location to visit since there are so many options. They strive to make their cruise an unforgettable experience for them. It was an accident they would never forget, full of fascinating and thrilling happenings.

For cruise ships, the Caribbean is one of the most popular locations. It is made up of various islands that may provide unique sailing opportunities. Nothing will compare to your experience here once you've tried it. For you, it was all a dream. Travel and cruise the Caribbean's beautiful waterways, covering kilometers of ocean that surrounds you and your other passengers. The sound of the wave crashing on the massive rocks along the shore will also be heard.

A Caribbean cruise is unquestionably pleasurable. The Caribbean Islands are a cruise ship's ideal destination. The square's islands are distinct from the rest of the islands since they are linked together. Because the islands are linked, you can hop from one to the next. Caribbean cruises are particularly fascinating because of their modernism, which is why you, as a contemporary nature lover, may easily become friends with them.

The cruise has a lot to offer in terms of fantastic experiences. You'll see rich greenery, lovely beaches, and lush green woods in this region. Despite the riches that can be seen in contemporary Caribbean resorts, you will still be able to enjoy the abundance of the areas' animal reserves. The temperature of the deep tropical rainforest, which can only be found in Puerto Rico and the vacation town of Bonaire, is tempting. The temperature is also unrivaled in any other location, making it ideal for swimming, visiting the beach, and snorkeling. From the outset, Caribbean cruises have been a popular destination for cruise ships.

The temperature on the island is warm, making it excellent for other beaches. The visible coral reefs will also amaze you, owing to the sea's crystal clear and pristine waters. Shopping is another draw on Caribbean cruises, in addition to the natural beauties that you will see. This is excellent news for individuals who like shopping. Purchasing the most desired mementos from your vacation is another enjoyable Caribbean activity. Shopping is certainly a fun thing to do while you're there. Because they are based on tax-free pricing, all of the prices are reasonable.

Caribbean Cruising offers a variety of itineraries to choose from. It's up to you to decide where you want to travel on a Caribbean journey and what you want to see. They may also provide you with a diverse variety of trip places, for example. For example, B. a two-day excursion or a longer one if you choose. Most Caribbean cruise lines choose to visit the islands for a longer period. They want to make the most of their time here since they need to return to the Caribbean for another season.

A multi-day Caribbean vacation provides you with a taste of the region's cultural diversity. You will also learn about the history of the Caribbean and the culture of the people who live there. Caribbean cruises, after all, are the most ideal for their families. Cruises to the Caribbean are a fantastic way to spend your children's summer holidays. This is the ideal opportunity to reconnect with your family and spend quality time with them while taking in the beauty of the Caribbean islands.

Carnival Cruises - Take a cruise trip with one of the world's most well-known cruise lines

Do you want to stop working eight hours a day, seven days a week? Is your daily routine monotonous, and you're looking for something fresh to sate your craving for adventure? So maybe all you need is three days or even a week on a Carnival cruise. This vacation is an excellent opportunity to spend a few days doing something positive for yourself.

You won't have to worry about spending extra for meals, entertainment, or other special activities while traveling. All you have to do now is unwind and carry your belongings aboard the boat. You will be treated by the personnel on board the ship, who will give you peaceful massages, spa saunas, hair treatments, and other cosmetic services. All of this may be found in one location; you simply need to visit each business to get the services.

Carnival Cruise Lines is one of the most well-known cruise lines in the world. The majority of tourists who are waiting to arrive at their destination eat, fantasize, and dance at all hours of the day and night. Carnival cruises are popular among first-time visitors, children and teenagers, young singles and older singles, couples, and adults. Casual eating at the Sea View Bistro, a handy 24-hour pizza, a Captain's Party, exquisite dining, and 24-hour room service are among the top Carnival cruise experiences.

You may also watch movies daily, bet in Las Vegas-style casinos, swim in onboard pools, buy in the duty-free shop, and sometimes attend parties. For all lone travelers, couples, and families, the Carnival Vacation is an entertainment-focused cruise. It draws a diverse range of tourists of all ages, and the ship's lifestyle is similar to that of any other cruise line.

You may also spend an evening abroad at one of the ship's cafés or restaurants, such as the Paris Lounge, the Café des Artistes, or the Casino de Monte Carlo. In addition to comprehensive luxury, a Carnival Cruise provides adequate room and pleasant accommodations in one of its cabins. Wardrobes and utilities such as basins, baths, and showers are provided in all cabins and bedrooms. Color television is also available in each bedroom. A Carnival cruise stateroom has all of the amenities that you would expect at home.

Rooms on Carnival Cruises are 50% bigger than those on other mid-size cruise lines, and you have 100% private space. If you are dissatisfied with Carnival Cruises' services, you may file a complaint with the cruise line. The cruise line is willing to refund the unused amount of the cruise fee as well as the cost of the return trip. So, what's the best way to get the best deal on a Carnival Cruise?

Obtain the services of a cruise professional

You may erase or at least decrease your questions and fears about employing a travel agency with the aid of a cruise specialist. Knowing how ships operate, the expert can determine the optimal date for a trip to a certain location. Cruise specialists can also provide information on cruise bargains, cruise locations, and cruise information. If you're searching for a cruise specialist, try to meet with them in person.

This guarantees that the expert you choose has gone on a trip previously and is familiar with the information you want. Additionally, when selecting a cruise specialist, ensure that the expert leads you through the booking process.

To be sure the expert isn't deceiving you, phone the shipping business and compare your estimate to the shipping firm's real pricing. Just double-check that the tariff includes all taxes and port fees. It makes little difference to most cruise vacationers how much a cruise holiday costs. Saving money, on the other hand, is quite essential to certain people. So, if you're one of those folks, you now know how to save money.

Carnival Cruise Lines offers a luxurious way to travel.

Cruising aboard cruise ships may be a fantastic way to travel. Many folks should think about considering cruise holidays. Relaxing travels to various sites across the globe, sampling international cuisines, and enjoying your holiday wherever your cruise takes you are all possibilities.

Imagine waking up to freshly prepared coffee and a delectable breakfast waiting for you at your breakfast table on a cruise. Step outdoors after breakfast to enjoy the sun or take in the magnificent surroundings on your journey to your destination. Then go for a dip in the pool or hot tub on the cruise ship.

After a refreshing dip in the pool, treat yourself to a soothing massage from the onboard masseuse. You may go to parties or bet at the onboard casinos in the evenings, and dine in style in your dining room. Then retire to your comfortable bedroom and plan your activities for the following day.

Cruise companies have a plethora of activities that enable you to relax and enjoy yourself. For days or maybe weeks, all you'll think about is resting in the sun. Carnival Cruise Lines is one of the most well-known cruise lines. They have one of the most entertaining floating resorts accessible in today's cruise holiday packages. They offer Carnival Exciting Ships, a floating resort with a variety of fun activities for people of all ages.

Carnival Cruise Ships provides a diverse range of locations. They provide cruises to both the United States and Europe. The following is a list of their cruise itineraries:

- Alaska

- Hawaii

- Mexico

- Panama Canal

- the Caribbean

- Bermuda

- Transatlantic

With so many options, you're guaranteed to enjoy the finest vacation of your life. Carnival Fun Ships provides a wide range of activities. The diversity of activities available will ensure that you do not get bored. Every night, they have a new themed party. They provide parties for older visitors with classical music, as well as gatherings for teenagers.

On a Carnival Fun Ship, you may enjoy the following activities and amenities:

• **Daytime Activities:** On a Carnival Fun Ship, daytime activities include golf lessons, use of the onboard pool and hot tubs, trying your luck at the casino, or just soaking up the sun and taking in the scenery.

• **Dining:** The Carnival Fun Ships provide first-class dining. They will give you fresh lobsters, superb wines, and other delights that you will undoubtedly like. They also provide informal eating, with buffets and other meals such as pizza, sushi, a European-style café, and other meals tailored to your preferences.

• **Spa:** Carnival Fun Ships include onboard spas and gyms. Carnival Fun Ships features excellent facilities and experts to assist you with your workout if you are too eager to rest and need to exercise. There are free weights and weight machines at the gym, as well as running track and aerobics sessions. They also feature a spa where you may have a peaceful massage from a trained therapist. The spas also provide cosmetic treatments for both men and women, ensuring that you always look your best while onboard.

• **Casino:** Do you have a fortunate streak? Onboard casinos are available aboard Carnival Fun Ships for you to try your luck. They provide casino services comparable to those found at a top-tier casino. Play slots, blackjack, poker, craps, and roulette to see whether you can win enough to cover the cost of the trip.

• **Camp Carnival:** Carnival Fun Ships also has kid-friendly activities. Bingo, cartoon time, face painting, recess, painting, and drawing competitions are among the activities available to children. There are activities for the younger ones, such as painting t-shirts, making doll shoes, playing outdoor games, and so on.

Table tennis, computer games, dancing courses, talent shows, and other sophisticated activities are available. Parties, games, swimming, meals, and late-night movies are all available to teenagers. There's also the O2 Club, where older kids may enjoy hip music, amazing movies, video games, teen shore excursions, teen lounges, and other fun activities to unwind.

Celebrity Cruises provides you with friendly and attentive service

Cruising the Caribbean may be more enjoyable when you are seated comfortably on a cruise line that can cater to your every need. One of the greatest cruise lines in the world is a cruise line. Visiting the whole Caribbean location is one method to round up your Caribbean trip. Does it seem to be impossible? Don't worry, with Celebrity Cruising Line, you won't have to. If you're new to traveling and don't know much about it, your best choice is to look up the finest cruise lines on the internet. The Celebrity Cruise is one of them.

Celebrity Cruises, according to records, gives the greatest service to its cruise lines in the United States and across the globe, particularly in the Caribbean Islands. This cruise company also offers five-star and six-star cruises. Imagine the kind of service they provide; the cruise company has even gone above and above on a few occasions. Cruises with Celebrity are fantastic! When surfing alongside celebrities, you may get a mixed benefits. It is designed uniquely. The cruise line's modernism will never be an issue for you. You can make the most of your resources; your journey will not be monotonous.

Celebrity Voyages, on the other hand, provides excellent service on all cruises. They provide you with the comfiest and reasonably priced chairs. It's only a matter of waiting for supper and savoring the delectable dishes on offer. Finally, if you need to recharge your batteries, they have a peaceful spa. This is one of their assets, and it draws a lot of cruise ships. It keeps you entertained while you're driving. The restaurant is one of the many appealing locations to visit aboard Celebrity Cruises. They are quite proud of the delectable meals they provide to their guests.

His delicacies have been praised by high-ranking visitors who have previously served them. Foodies are also quite appreciative of the foods they create. They've also earned several culinary honors for the greatest cuisine and chefs they've hired. A celebrity cruise is appealing for a variety of reasons. The long connection between them and the passengers, in addition to their highly valued customized treatment, the recognized services that they give that are not found by other cruise lines in the globe, the large areas that they make accessible to tourists for their lodging...

Most cruise companies, predictably, choose celebrity cruises since they provide their passengers with so many amenities that are valued above all else. Your recordings will be preserved after you board your ships. Celebrity Cruises maintains its reputation with its consumers for a longer period by maintaining high standards across the board. He tries to make things flawless as much as possible. They anticipate each client's demands to reply quickly to their requests. Get what you need as soon as possible. On celebrity cruises, one staff person is usually hired for every two passengers. To put it another way, they are always available. They can also accommodate your requirements. You don't have to put forth a lot of effort to attain them.

The staff is also friendly. Celebrity Cruises workers are dedicated to offering its passengers exceptional European hospitality and courteous service. They hire the greatest service personnel, who are always eager to help. The crew has undergone extensive training to ensure that only the finest service is provided. The cruise ships are likewise pampered by the management. Chefs must be original and creative.

Aside from delicious cuisine, the presentation must be flawless. The taste has to be fantastic. So, if you're considering a Caribbean trip, don't waste time deciding which cruise company is ideal. Celebrity Cruises has all of your needs covered. Celebrity Cruises will make your Caribbean trip an unforgettable experience! Good luck and have a good time!

Celebrity Cruise Line offers an all-inclusive holiday

How will you spend your week off if you had one?
Of course, you want to reward yourself with something special; after all, you want to relax and unwind after a long day at work.

Immersion? Escalation?
Do you travel with a rucksack on your back? There are many things to select from, but make sure you have a budget-friendly and quick vacation. When it comes to diving, for example, you must locate the greatest dive locations both inside and outside the United States. Mountaineering is the same way.

It's a waste of time since you won't be able to reach the summit in a single day of climbing. When traveling with a backpack, you must pack and unload at each hotel; at the same time, you must locate restaurants and other necessities using a travel card.

Consider taking a cruise for an inexpensive and short vacation. You don't have to do this while browsing, just like the Get-It-All Getaways above. The cruise ships include all of the facilities you might desire (gym, restaurants, swimming pools, casino).

You won't have to worry about your baggage; just check it in and it will be immediately kept in your suite after you've checked in. The parade of delectable cuisine that passes through the dining halls of cruise ships is also a highlight of cruise activities. Each cruise ship has its restaurant, which is overseen by some of the world's greatest chefs. These rides are all included in the cruise price, so you won't have to take money out of your pocket to enjoy them.

During your local tourism activities, guides are present at each port to help you. You don't have to be concerned about your children; there are a variety of things you may engage in while working on your company. A cruise trip allows you to savor every moment of your holiday while also relieving you of the stress of travel.

The aforementioned amenities are available on all cruise lines, however, you must have at least one for your holiday. This article will enlighten you about Celebrity Cruise Line and why you should consider them as one of your alternatives when deciding which cruise line to sail with. Celebrity Cruise Line is one of the world's greatest cruise lines. They provide a cost-effective bundle that includes access to information forums about your chosen region.

Cirque du Soleil planned and constructed opulent Las Vegas-style stores and onboard entertainment specifically for Celebrity. You may try your luck at the casino or even purchase works of art at the onboard auction. If you can't sleep at night, go to The Bar at the Edge of the Earth, a Celebrity-owned exotic club.

Visit the renowned Elemis Aqua-Spa if you wish to unwind. You'll find beautiful manicures, facials, and relaxing massages here. If you wish to feel rejuvenated and energized, the Celebrity also features an acupuncture clinic on board. Your children will have a great time on the trip. Celebrity has created the X-Club youth program just for your kids. It caters to a certain age group with activities and entertainment. All of these events, including scientific and naturalistic inquiry, scavenger hunts, talent performances, feasts, and more, are overseen by expert professionals.

Celebrity has designated some places of the ship for young sailors, such as the Shipmates Fun Factory, the youth center, and the swimming pools. So that your kids may enjoy their activities while on cultural trips. It's not only for kids and adults to go on cruises. It's also a great place to visit if you have a disability. Celebrity ships have been developed to accommodate travelers with limited mobility. Some workers are always available to assist you with your medical and other requirements.

Celebrity also has an onboard clinic with a qualified doctor and a nurse that can also communicate in another language. You are in charge of the passengers' health on board. In canteens and dining rooms, food is offered 24 hours a day. If you want to have a romantic supper with your spouse or wife, you may book room service. Every night, there is also a formal supper for individuals who wish to show off their best outfits and jewels.

Finally, travel routes for the cruise destination are arranged. the epoch itself You may borrow the ship for the whole day to travel or disembark. You may go back to any place as long as you return to the ship as soon as possible after leaving. Optional activities are also available. Simply contact the transportation provider ahead of time to organize an appointment. With the Celebrity Clinee Cruise, you may enjoy the crocodile!

Disney cruises are a dream come true for many people

Disney Land is a magical and entertaining realm. It's a great location to celebrate holidays, birthdays, and other special occasions. But, most importantly, it's a beautiful location where your children may have the time of their lives as you reconnect with your inner child.

Disney Cruises offers a magnificent but economical way to experience the wonder of Disney Land. There are numerous kinds of resort accommodations at Walt Disney World Resort. Rooms should ideally be near the embarkation point. Deluxe cabins are also available on the cruise ship's balcony.

All guests are allowed to shop in the cruise ship's stateroom. This is just one of the many advantages that a Disney cruise can provide. The traveler may take in various magnificent vistas on the trip to the Disney Wonder. For example, the passenger may make a pit break at the gangway area to shoot photographs. The passenger may also relax for a few hours on the navigation table. As a consequence, the passenger may travel in excellent comfort and relaxation.

The majority of cruise lines that visit Disney Wonder make a significant influence. In most lines, there are a variety of eateries to choose from. Many different cuisines are available on cruise ships. The majority of the food is imported from various regions of the globe. There's also infant food available.

Mountain shrimp, sliced meats, superb desserts, a variety of salads, and lively tropical drinks make up the majority of the cuisine served at their magnificent banquets and menus. Children's meals are also available to please your children's palates. Many amenities are available in the ship's aft, where passengers may spend their excess time. A pool terrace is also a great place for kids to play.

Relax and rest in one of the many comfy armchairs strewn across the room. There are also sunbathing areas. Aside from that, the passenger has adequate time on board to play table tennis and other sports. A Disney cruise is an unforgettable family vacation. Every room on most cruise ships has a television. The traveler may bring a lot of baggage in the cabin with this equipment. Not only that but if the passenger books the trip in advance, the shipping company may be able to offer them discounts and special offers. Even meal menus are included in the carefully ordered bundled with typical arrangements.

Aside from that, each guest may take use of spa services. Passengers' class timings are usually noted as they arrive. The majority of the road leading to Disney World is labeled "Part Sail Away." It's where the traveler will meet at the end of the day when he departs. Many entertainment packages are available at Sail Away Part. Every night, there are dancing and circus shows. In addition, there are Disney characters to be found.

Passengers may also pose with Mickey Mouse and his buddies for family pictures. At all times, boat photographers are available. You are in charge of photographing every component of the yacht. Passengers may often see and buy the recorded image. There are various picture bundles to choose from. Passengers may purchase these packages to capture the greatest images of their vacation and preserve their memories forever.

Additionally, Disney Cruises provides a unique method of food preparation. There are three different meal options on the menu. Passengers may choose from a variety of fresh menus and meals every day. For example, the first evening's meal may have Animators Pilates, while the following day's menu might include Tritons; each day brings a new and exciting stomach journey.

On a Disney cruise, passengers may choose their favorite activity schedule for the whole day. Not only that, but Disney World offers a wide range of ground activities. Choosing the best organization is the most challenging aspect of the scenario. But, at their core, these activities are delightful to partake in. This fascinating cruise is an excellent opportunity to unwind with the kids. Disney Cruises is certain to provide the greatest cruise experience possible. Excitement, entertainment, and leisure are all rolled into one. Disney is both a place of enchantment and imagination, as well as a place of realism.

Disney Cruise Line - For the Happiness of Your Child

It is more than a chance to spend time with your children. You always want the best for your children as a parent. It doesn't matter how much money you spend as long as you provide an outstanding experience. Spending your childhood is just a once-in-a-lifetime opportunity, so make the most of it. The sky was so clear that it was pitch black. Even the stars are bright; the ocean is slowly flowing, and the atmosphere is serene. We can hear the kids giggling hysterically.

Can you imagine a holiday like this aboard a cruise ship? Isn't it enough for you?

When it comes to having fun with your kids, cruises are one of the finest options. Allow them to go on a cruise to see the marvels of the globe. It will provide your family with an experience they have never experienced before in terms of pleasure and excitement. The pleasures of traveling are not limited to professionals and independent people who vacation during the cruise season.

Cruise lines, on the other hand, provide possibilities for young individuals who want to get a taste of what it's like to work in the industry. The Disney Cruise Line is the only cruise line that has special programming for children. When parents desire to take their children on a trip, it has been selected as the top cruise line.

The same delusions that may be found in Disneyland can be found here. They amuse youngsters with pets that are often seen in Disneyland. You'll have a lot of fun searching with these animated creatures. Furthermore, children of all ages are welcome to participate in the program, games, and activities. They will not be bored by the journey since they will have access to all of the Disney cruise line's entertainment options. It not only makes them laugh, but it also makes them delighted about their vacation.

The Disney cruise line's vacation season is often regarded as its high point. This is the time of year when a lot of bookings need to be made. The number of parents who get reservations might sometimes reach millions. After a month of busy school events, this is perhaps the ideal method for them to offer their children some leisure time.

Offer activities for teens such as storytelling, drawing, and sometimes simply having fun while playing. This is appropriate for children under the age of seven, particularly small youngsters. They do, however, provide unique activities for practically all teens. They have arcade games, mini-parties with board games, and so on. Here you may discuss ideas with your fellow passengers.

For parents who wish to take their children on a cruise, the Disney Company offers two enormous ships. Disney Magic is the first, while Disney Wonder is the second. The majority of cruise ship services are available here, just as they are on any other cruise ship.

They also provide guests with the greatest dishes that their restaurants have to offer. In certain restaurants, there are also entertainment shows that you may watch while eating. The Disney Magic and Disney Wonder cruises have different design concepts. However, their services are unparalleled, since both can provide you with the pleasure you want not just for your children but your whole family.

The cruise company also features isolated spots onboard that are suited for everyone. Teenagers and adults have separate areas. It's a technique to make the most of the fun, the activities for the kids, and the social lives of these people's parents. However, don't expect to find everything you'll discover at Disneyland on the Disney Cruise Line, even if the ambiance and pleasure are almost identical. So, what exactly are you waiting for? Now is an excellent time to spend quality time with your children.

Make it a memorable event for you and your friends to discuss when they return to their towns! Enjoy your Disney Cruise Line cruise journey!

Spend Your Cruise To Your Dream Destination With Hawaii Cruises

Who hasn't fantasized about visiting Hawaii? Of course, everyone fantasizes about visiting Hawaii and spending their holiday there. For many individuals, Hawaii has become a fantasy vacation location. Tourists and cruise ships alike like visiting these distinctive holiday destinations. The four Hawaiian islands might be an excellent location for your large Hawaii cruise. These distinct islands are beautiful and charming in their own right. Your voyage to the four separate islands of Maui, Kauai, Oahu, and the Big Island will undoubtedly be enjoyable.

When arranging a cruise, you should make an effort to visit these locations. Hawaii vacations are ideal for those who work hard all year. You will not only view the island of Hawaii on a Hawaii cruise, but you will also have the chance to explore the whole state. Hawaii's wonderful climate allows visitors to come at any time of year. It's an excellent vacation place.

All you have to do now is determine which cruise to take, but with so many cruise lines to choose from, this will never be a problem. As long as you choose a cruise that has everything you need at a reasonable cost. You will be met by a plethora of activities as soon as your foot onto the table. Inside the boat, there are a plethora of entertaining features. The many entertainment facilities, spas, boutiques, swimming pools, and even sports centers are guaranteed to please.

You will undoubtedly appreciate the many pubs and clubs on the table if you are a highly open-minded individual. You may go to the café or read your favorite books at the library if you want to relax. On your Hawaii cruise, you will undoubtedly never be bored. The smallest and most distant of the Big Island is Kauai, popularly known as "Garden Island." The rich culture and fauna will captivate you. On Kauai, there are many gorgeous spots to visit that provide a variety of outdoor activities. Cycling, sightseeing, picnics, eating, and off-road adventures are just a few of the various activities that may be enjoyed there.

Kauai is well-known for its unusual island formation. When Hollywood filmmakers attempt to depict some of Hawaii's natural fauna, they frequently shoot their films here. Begin with Waimea Canyon, which may be reached through a long journey across the island. You may also go to Oahu, Hawaii's second-largest island, for a day trip. This unique island is home to the world-famous Waikiki Beach.

Oahu is recognized for its main island, which has long been a popular dating spot. This is an excellent spot for a Hawaii cruise. You may enjoy all of the conveniences and pleasures of visiting each island. You may dive in the deep waters of Pearl Harbor, learn about its fascinating history, and sail across the island, stopping at the Polynesian Cultural Center to learn about Hawaii's fascinating past.

There's also the option of going to Maui. Many outdoor activities, including kayaking, riding, and mountain bike trips, are available on this island. This unique location is home to some of the nicest beaches in the world. The summit of Haleakala is a must-see tourist attraction. Finally, you'll go to the biggest of the four islands, the Big Island, popularly known as Hawaii. You will learn a lot more about this island than you will about the other islands available.

You may take participate in a variety of outdoor activities and visit the fascinating Hawaii Volcanoes, National Park. There is enough magnificent landscape to spend your time doing anything you want, wherever you want to go and whatever you want to do. When you visit Hawaii aboard a cruise ship, you may experience all of these things. You'll also find a variety of landscapes and rich Hawaiian history, as well as nature's stunning beauty, which will keep you going back. You simply have to be cautious since land cruising in Hawaii may become addictive.

A Mediterranean cruise is a fantastic way to spend your vacation

Are you considering taking a cruise but aren't sure where you'll go? Read this post to find out where the greatest location is. While reading it, you may be sure to acquire the greatest hint. Cruises are boat outings that take place on sailboats or motorboats.

Traveling and vacationing take more than days; it takes years. It is not a simple journey that lasts simply a week or two. Cruises take a long time since traveling to various areas of the earth takes just a few minutes. Traveling across the globe takes three to 10 years. However, if there is a precise location, it may just take years or even weeks. On a Mediterranean Sea cruise, this is one of the most popular destinations.

Only a portion of the nation has access to the Mediterranean Sea, which is part of the Atlantic Ocean. Europe, South Africa, and East Asia are all affected. It is a large sea, covering over 2.5 million square kilometers. It is most often referred to as the Eurasian Mediterranean or the European Mediterranean.

The Mediterranean cruise is the most popular in the world. It features more than 120 seaports along the coast, with cruise services and vacation packages ranging from a week to longer holiday vacations. On your Mediterranean cruise, you will undoubtedly encounter a variety of cultures by visiting the location. You will undoubtedly go to seventeen countries with diverse cultures, like Spain, Greece, Egypt, and Italy.

Each of these destinations has its unique culture and attractions, making them the ideal incentive to visit them on your trip. Sail across the clear Mediterranean waters. Mediterranean cruises are available from a variety of firms. There are more than 50 firms from which to pick. The majority of these firms specialize in Western Mediterranean cruises, where you may select between Spain, France, Morocco, and Portugal.

Other cruise lines provide Eastern Mediterranean trips to Greece, Croatia, Turkey, and other Middle Eastern locations. You have the option of going to the nations of Cyprus and Malta as well. You'll also visit nations in North Africa.

If you choose a lengthier trip rather than a cruise, you will be able to visit more countries, including that outside of the Mediterranean. You will not only enjoy the voyage, but you will also admire the many landscapes, cultures, and customs encountered along the way. During your voyage, you will enjoy learning about diverse tales, amazing cities, ancient monuments, charming islands, stunning scenery, and different people.

You may also opt to travel to the western Mediterranean throughout your voyage, docking in classic Andalusian white villages in southern Spain. You may also come in contact with Cadiz's well-known sherry, Manzanilla. Your Western Mediterranean cruise will take you to Barcelona, the French Riviera, and other European sites. You'll also arrive at the lovely coast, which is home to treasures like the extinct volcano Vesuvius, ancient Pompeii, and Rome's charming city. It is also feasible to go to the Italian islands of Sicily and Sardinia.

Your trip to the Western Mediterranean will be remembered for these breathtaking vistas. The various views of Italy and other countries in the western Mediterranean will undoubtedly appeal to you. The final region of the sea that you will explore is the Eastern Mediterranean. The stunning Croatian coast will undoubtedly delight you. Before diving into the classic and sultry island of Greece, you'll see the charming and beautiful city of Dubrovnik.

Crete is the island often visited on a Mediterranean cruise, where the Knossos spectacle is just a stone's throw away. You will never forget this event on your Mediterranean cruise holiday. If you want to learn more about cruising in the Mediterranean, visit a few sites on the Internet. You can collect information using the various search engines available on the Internet.

Norwegian Cruise Lines invites you to have a cruise vacation onboard

Your employer grants you a week off after a long week at work to unwind and enjoy a vacation. You have a variety of alternatives, such as trekking and discovering new locations or diving and marveling at the marine environment's magnificence.

A boat tour is an excellent choice for a holiday or a pleasant travel destination. While viewing the majesty of the Atlantic waves, you may sip your favorite lemon juice. Relax along the clean water's edge, where you can view everything it has to offer without diving in. You will have a great time sailing over your holiday week. This sort of holiday activity is available on several cruise lines. Cruise lines are situated in both Europe and America. Norwegian Cruise Lines may be the finest alternative for you if you choose to cruise the country's waterways.

Norwegian Cruise Line was created in 1966 by Knut Kloster and Ted Arison and is based in Miami, Florida. It all began with an 830-ton steamer that conducted Caribbean trips, which was later purchased by France, who converted it into a cruise ship and renamed it Norway. The success of Norway opened the path for NCL's success with the world's largest cruise lines. NCL's fleet now consists of eleven huge, contemporary cruise ships. Norwegian Star, the most opulent cruise ship, sails to Alaska in the summer and the Mexican Riviera in the winter.

Her most recent ship, the Norwegian Spirit, follows similar itineraries as the Star, except in the winter, she travels across the Caribbean through the Panama Canal. If you want to cruise Hawaii, choose NCL's Pride of Aloha, which specializes in Hawaiian Island cruises.

In the meanwhile, the Norwegian Dawn departs New York for destinations in Florida and the Caribbean. From Houston, the Norwegian Sea reaches the Caribbean. The Norwegian Majesty also cruises to ports in Mexico and the Bahamas in the Caribbean. NCL's 20-year-old cruise ship, the Norwegian Crown, can accommodate 2,000 passengers and provides a much more intimate setting for classic cruising experiences.

NCL has turned the typical cruising experience into a unique and much more intimate one since introducing the Freestyle concept in 2000. Freestyle Cruising is a cruise line that caters to the demands of its guests. It provides passengers with a resort-style cruise experience with plenty of personal freedom. NCL also boasts the largest ratio of cruise workers to passengers of any cruise line, and its customers get the finest treatment. Aside from its size and elegant style, your spacecraft shines in every way. The cheerful and polite cruise crew will always greet you in the hallway, ready to assist you with everything you want.

NCL's voyages include Freestyle Dining, which is one of the company's hallmarks. Food on board used to be a "fixed affair," with meals served at set times, allotted dining chairs, and a proper dress code. You may pick from a dozen different dining locations at NCL Freestyle Dining and dine whenever you wish. Some dining rooms are designed in such a way that the food is already cooked. There is no dress requirement; just put on your jeans, grab a tray, and choose your favorite meals.

Menu-based meals are served in the main dining room, so make sure you have dressed appropriately for supper. The cruise ticket includes all meals served in these dining rooms. Food presentation isn't always what it seems to be. Believe it or not, a weeklong cruise trip might cause you to gain an average of seven pounds! On each ship, NCL also serves a selection of premium meals or delicacies.

Chinese, French, or Italian foods, for example, are offered in tiny, well-decorated restaurants. You will be charged an extra fee if you want a gourmet restaurant. Don't worry, however. You'll get a lot more than your money. NCL provides a range of onboard activities 24 hours a day, in addition to its exquisite dining service. If you wish to stay in shape while on vacation, you may work out in the fully equipped gym regularly.

They also feature several cafes and nightclubs where great artists play every night in case you can't sleep. Theatrical entertainment includes anything from stand-up comedy to Las Vegas plays. This isn't essential if you lose your game experience. You can visit its stunning casino, which has slot machines and other slot machines while cruising on the sea. Try Norwegian Cruise Lines and see what a difference it makes.

Escape to paradise with Princess Cruises

Do you wish to take a vacation to get away from your hectic lifestyle?
Have you ever wished to make a difference on your final trip while still flying?
Have you ever wished for a memorable family vacation?
Do you want to go on another honeymoon with your wife?

If you answered yes to any of these questions, a cruise is most likely the ideal way to spend your holiday. Imagine sunbathing, getting a massage, eating a beautiful supper, resting by the pool, working out in the gym, and taking a pleasant break while going to your destination. additional things you believe are difficult to do throughout your journey When you arrange your cruise trip, you may do all of this.

People choose cruise lines for their holidays because of the convenience they provide. Cruises are similar to floating hotels in that they provide all of the amenities of a high-end hotel. Unlike aircraft, which have limited room, cruise ships provide an alternative mode of transportation. You arrive at your destination well-rested and unwinded.

Some cruise lines promise to give excellent service. Princess Cruise Lines is one of them. This shipping firm promises to provide a unique cruise experience. It provides excellent service and a diverse range of activities for travelers. Princess Cruise Lines is now one of the most popular cruise lines in the world. They provide a wide range of cruises to several places all around the globe. Princess Cruise Lines offers the following destinations:

Alaska

Europe

Asia

Australia's Hawaii and Tahiti

New England and Canada

Riviera de México

Canal de Panama in the Caribbean

South America is a continent in South America

You'll have a lot of options for vacation places since there are so many different sites to see. You may also have difficulty picking which one to chose since these locations provide a variety of attractions, cruise options, and prices. Choose the one that appeals to you the most.

Imagine waking up each morning to a magnificent new perspective of the globe if you're new to the world of cruise ships and don't know what to anticipate. Wouldn't it be nice to be pampered at a five-star resort? The cost of a Princess Cruises trip includes lodging, food, entertainment, use of the ship's amenities, individual service from a Princess Cruises staffer for three guests, access to the casino, and more.

There are other services offered for a fee, but it would be worth it to get the most out of the pleasure and relaxation. Princess Cruises also provides the following additional services:

- *a full-service spa with massage treatment*
- *auctions*
- *bar beverages*
- *former*
- *24-hour childcare service*
- *beauty salon*
- *purchases*
- *beach trips*

Packages for singles are also available. The Love Boat Singles Cruise is a Princess Cruise unique for singles, with special drinks, mixers, games, cuisine, and more. A Singles Cruise is an excellent chance to meet new people and form new friendships. Every day may be different on a Princess cruise ship since there are so many facilities. With the ship's amenities, you may have a good time every day. You may spend your time on the green golfing, swimming, and other activities.

There is also a children's club where your children may play in the arcades or socialize with the other members of the team. Your cruise trip is just the beginning of your holiday. There are organized beach excursions to the locations where your cruise ship docks that take you inland. You'll be able to learn about the cultures of the ports you visit, examine the animals, trek on a glacier, and go shopping.

A Princess Voyage consultant will guide you through the intricacies of a particular cruise if you are unsure which Princess cruise is perfect for you. You may let the personnel know about your cruise requirements, interests, and expectations. Princess Cruises provides several different packages. If you are a first-time Princess Cruise passenger, this is the best option. Whether you're single, bringing your family on vacation, or taking your wife on her honeymoon, a Princess Cruise holiday ensures the utmost in luxury and excitement.

With the Princess Cruises fleet, you may travel to more places

Remember the Disney Princesses Island Princess and Pacific Princess? These are the cruise lines featured in the popular television show The Love Boat, which aired from 1977 to 1986.

Inside the ship, the passengers and crew had a romantic and enjoyable adventure with luxurious and enjoyable amenities. If you assume these boats are just extras for the series, you're mistaken. Princess Cruises, an American cruise business, owned both of these cruise lines. Princess Cruises stands out among the major shipping lines in the cruise industry since it travels to many cruise destinations around the world.

Is that the case?

When Stanley MacDonald chartered Princess Patricia, a ferry operated by Canadian Pacific Limited, for cruises sailing from Los Angeles in the mid-1960s, Princess Cruises was born. Princess Pat, on the other hand, was never intended to travel in tropical climates. Her charter was cut short in favor of a cruise to Italy. Italy was one of the first cruise lines to include modern design aspects into its ships, such as lifeboats that were positioned further aft. Allows you to put the boat motor in the stern and create a wide public area.

However, its creators and owners fell bankrupt after it was built. The princess purchased Italy after it was sold to a bank. Princess renamed herself Princess Italia and utilized it for Alaska cruises departing from San Francisco. The charter was canceled in 1973, and the ship was returned to Europe for Costa Cruise Line charter trips. Carla von Costa is her third charter cruise ship. She was bought right after she was rebuilt in the late 1960s. She was renamed Princess Carla after being chartered to Princess. Princess Carla appears in certain Love Boat TV series scenes with the Sun Princess, which the Princess purchased from Norwegian Cruise Lines.

The Princess transport fleet was bolstered in 1974 with the acquisition of Sea Venture and Island Venture from Flagship Cruises, which would subsequently become Pacific Princess and Island Princess. The Kungsholm, a former Swedish liner owned by Flagship Cruises, is the Princess' seventh ship. It was renamed Sea Princess after its engineers and naval designers renovated and restored it in Bremen. The Royal Princess, the company's ninth ship, was the first purpose-built cruise ship. She was one of the first British liners to ship without any internal cabins when she debuted in 1984.

Sitmar Line was also acquired by Princess in 1988, and all of its ships were transferred to the Princess fleet. In 1990, the Crown Princess and the Regal Princess joined the Princess fleet of ten luxury cruise lines, bringing the total to ten. Princess distinguishes itself from other cruise lines by sailing via popular destinations such as Alaska, the Caribbean, Hawaii, Mexico, and the Panama Canal, as previously indicated. It turns out that it is the greatest cruise package supplier at a reasonable price. They strive to provide their consumers with the luxury of a cruise without breaking the bank.

Dance lessons, sporting activities, spa treatment facilities, nighttime entertainment, and a range of onboard activities are all available on the Princess series of ships. You do not need to be bored. You will take part in a variety of activities while having a good time. They also serve both classic and modern meals, allowing you to consume your favorite foods wherever and whenever you want. Princess Cruises offers Caribbean cruises- If you prefer a Caribbean cruise, they also offer various possibilities.

To be accurate, there are three options. The Eastern Caribbean, Southern Caribbean, and the Western Caribbean are the three alternatives. Charlotte Amalie and Saint-Martin are two sites to explore while your cruise ship is docked. Stopovers in other locations of the Caribbean are also possible. Snorkeling and diving, driving, and fishing are just a few of the activities available in the Caribbean.

It's the ideal location for doing a variety of activities or doing nothing at all. Princess Cruises offers shore excursions, or you can go on your own and explore them. There are a variety of other reasons to embark on a Princess Cruise. Try it out for yourself and embark on amazing cruises.

Royal Caribbean Cruises offer a luxurious way to visit the island

Only if we carry out our conservation strategy will the earth become a great paradise...

It gives me tremendous pleasure and honor to be able to show others around the world how lovely the world can be through the natural beauty of the Caribbean. The long-chain island, with its animals, green meadows, and culturally minded people, is one of the most beautiful sights in the Caribbean. The Caribbean's attractions will dazzle you beyond your wildest dreams. It's more than just a surf spot; it's a true melting pot of humanity. It's a seductive invention, the ideal location to dwell despite all of life's challenges. This is the place to go if you need a break.

There's nothing wrong with a little daydreaming now and then. "Sir, lady, may we bring you something?" imagines a sailor on a luxury yacht. The customer service is outstanding. When the sun shines, you'll be offered a steaming coffee, delectable seafood for lunch, and a white wine punch in the evening. You'll be treated as if you're a king or queen.

Surfing in the Caribbean is one of those once-in-a-lifetime experiences that you will never forget. The Caribbean country welcomes you with shimmering sand, azure ocean, and a great area of green and fertile terrain. You will find that exploring the Caribbean is a worthwhile activity. While traveling around the country's small islands, there are several discoveries to be made. You can even broaden your geographic understanding of why things are the way they are in the Caribbean.

The Caribbean is situated between Mexico's southern suburbs and Venezuela's northwestern region. As a result, the people who dwell on the island have diverse cultural backgrounds. When planning a trip to the Caribbean, consider a variety of factors, including the type of cruise package you want to take. In the Caribbean, there are two major cruise ships. The Eastern Caribbean Cruise and the Southern Caribbean Cruise are the two options.

The first package allows you to explore the Eastern Caribbean's beauty. The British and American Isles, as well as the Bahamas, Puerto Rico, and St. Martin, are all located here. The cold and humid paradises of Antiqua, Barbados, Aruba, Saint Kitts, and Granada can be found in the south. Starting with a standard seven-day package, you can prolong the duration of your trip if you wish to see the entire Caribbean.

Exploring the Long Chain Islands takes a long time

The nice part about Alaska Cruise's packages is that they cater to all budgets. If you're looking for a low-cost option, a package is a way to go. It all depends on how long your trip is and what kind of service you pick. The Royal Caribbean Cruise is the most luxurious and magnificent of all cruises. It is regarded as one of the top cruises in the world, capable of providing enticing cruise service. Although a Royal Caribbean Cruise is pricey, it provides first-class service.

Most Caribbean cruises also provide a variety of nighttime entertainment for their passengers. You also have the option of visiting the above-mentioned destinations, which are not included in the economy package. There is no doubt about the delicious treats they can provide you with, as well as the comfortable seat they will provide you with. On a Royal Caribbean cruise, the nightlife is quite different.

You'll mingle with your peers and meet the other exceptional individuals who are also looking forward to the vacation to the gorgeous islands. Your fantasy will come true with a Royal Caribbean Cruise. Try to take a Caribbean cruise to gain a better understanding of the natural beauty of the Caribbean islands. Best of luck and safe travels!

Why should you book a cruise with Royal Caribbean?

Cruising is one of the most luxurious holiday options available to you and your family. The thought of traveling to majestic and wonderful sites on a cruise is excellent for a holiday, even if it is meant to be opulent (which is synonymous with pricey). Several cruise lines cater to wealthy and middle-aged passengers with a choice of cruise packages.

If you're considering a cruise holiday, Royal Caribbean Cruise Lines is a great option. They have a large range of vacation goodies and selections for you. They are one of the most well-known cruise companies, and the amenities they provide to passengers on board the ship are excellent.

If you're unfamiliar with Royal Caribbean Cruise Line, you might believe that their ships solely travel to the Caribbean. While the Caribbean is included in its cruise itineraries, it also visits Alaska, Bermuda, Bahamas, Hawaii, Europe, Mexico, Canada, the Pacific Northwest, the Panama Canal, and transatlantic ports. They also provide fantastic cruises, which include an escorted shore excursion either before or after the cruise.

It's run by a first-class coach or train, and it allows you to view more of the country you're visiting. Royal Caribbean International, situated in Miami, Florida, operates Royal Caribbean Cruise Lines. There are now 19 ships in service, with two more on the way. Their ships all have names that end in "of the Seas."

Each of their ships features an exclusive club, known as the Viking Crown Lounge, located at the very top of the ship and offering panoramic views. It also offers a children's program called Adventure Ocean on board.

So, what are the best Royal Caribbean Cruise Lines offers to its passengers?

The informational speeches regarding your location and the ship itself come first. Throughout the voyage, you will be led to various onboard amenities such as ice rinks and an onboard casino. Your typical Las Vegas pachinko game will not be missed. Why don't you try relaxing your entire body? Onboard, there is a massage center and spa that will help you relax. An acupuncture center is also available, where you may learn about Chinese massage and the healing procedure.

Royal Caribbean Cruise Lines also offers the Adventure Ocean Youth program for your children, as previously mentioned. For the little ones, there are Fisher-Price Aqua Babies and Aqua-Tots. Onboard, there is a kid-friendly climbing wall that will keep your children entertained while they interact with other children. On a land tour, they will be responsible for their activities.

Cruises are not an issue for the crippled or old. Its cruises are tailored to the needs of clients who are old or have limited mobility. Employees on cruise ships are also available to assist you. On all of their ships, there are also medical services for everyone on board, including an emergency clinic with CPR equipment. An English-speaking doctor and nurses look after this.

When you board Royal Caribbean Cruise Lines, culinary activities are a huge draw. They have a broad variety of Italian, Mediterranean, and European cuisines available in their dining rooms, both the cafeteria and the main dining room.

It is simple to book a cruise. Simply register with internet travel agencies and request that they plan a cruise for you. You can also visit the Royal Caribbean Cruise Line's official website. They provide various discounts and incredible offers to fill in the gaps on the ship. There are fantastic offers on any trip you choose, whether you book early or late.

There's no excuse not to include Royal Caribbean Cruise Lines on your next cruise holiday with their pleasant, first-class service and inexpensive costs.

Chapter -16

How to Take a Luxury Cruise Around the World

Sailing across the globe may seem to be an unachievable ambition, but it is far more achievable than you may imagine. Cruises allow you to travel to every continent in style while enjoying the convenience of five-star service and entertainment. If you're interested in reaching this unique travel goal, the website details all of the ways you can sail around the globe on a luxury cruise.

North America is located in North America: Begin your voyage with a cruise to the Pacific Northwest in the United States, then sail down the New England and Canadian coasts, stop in Charleston on a Bermuda cruise, or cruise from Florida to the Caribbean.

Cruises to Alaska, America's Last Frontier, are among our most popular North American itineraries. Celebrity Cruises has cruises departing from Seattle, Washington, Vancouver, British Columbia, and Seward, Alaska. See spectacular natural marvels like Hubbard Glacier and Dawes Glacier on an Alaska cruise, as well as exciting ports of call like Juneau, Ketchikan, and Icy Strait Point.

The Caribbean is a beautiful place: Caribbean cruises stop at several island spots if you wish to go to someplace more exotic (and probably warmer). On a Western Caribbean cruise, see the white-sand beaches of Cozumel and the eccentric town of Key West. Visit the gorgeous ABC islands of Aruba, Bonaire, and Curacao in the southern Caribbean. On an Eastern Caribbean cruise, see the magnificent pitons of St. Lucia or enjoy a swim at Magens Bay in St. Thomas.

South America is a continent in South America: Cruises to South America are a fantastic opportunity to discover the wonders of the Southern Hemisphere. Take a sail around the southern point of the continent to Chile, Argentina, and Uruguay, or go to Peru and Brazil.

Galapagos blue-footed boobies: The Galapagos Islands, which are rich in exotic animals and surreal natural beauties, are one of the greatest spots to visit if you're traveling on a luxury cruise around the globe. You'll sail around the islands with an onboard naturalist who will explain to you about the sea lions, giant tortoises, marine lizards, and amazing birds you'll see along the way on your Galapagos tour.

Europe: Without a visit to the interesting content of Europe, no trip around the globe is complete. Enjoy the cuisine, wine, and culture of major towns and beach villages in Italy, Spain, France, and Greece on an amazing Mediterranean cruise trip.

Sail across the Baltic Sea to the nations of Scandinavia and the northern coastlines of Germany, Belgium, and Russia for something a bit different. Visit historic ports of call in England, Scotland, and Ireland as you travel throughout the United Kingdom. With so many options, you could decide to take many European cruises before moving on to the next continent on your agenda.

Asia: If you've always wanted to visit Asia to stroll along the Great Wall of China, see the glories of India, or explore the islands of Southeast Asia, Celebrity Cruises has you covered with a selection of multi-country cruise itineraries.

Sail throughout Asia on a luxury cruise and enjoy the convenience of seeing numerous cities and countries in one holiday. Join a guided tour trip to learn about the culture and history of Japan, Vietnam, Malaysia, the Philippines, India, and other countries.

Australia, New Zealand, and the South Pacific are all part of the South Pacific region: Explore the Southern Hemisphere on one of our Australia and New Zealand tours. In ports like Tauranga and Picton, you may take in the rich natural splendor of New Zealand. Choose an itinerary that takes you to the South Pacific's unique islands, such as Bora Bora, Fiji, and the legendary Mystery Island. Explore Australia's world-famous beaches, wine region, and the major ports of Sydney and Melbourne to round off your journey.

Africa: Agadir, Morocco, is a stop on several cruises between Europe and the United States. While knocking Africa off your cruise bucket list, enjoy the golden sand beaches and busy marketplaces of this main resort town.

Antarctica: On an extraordinary cruise holiday, go to the world's southernmost continent. Elephant Island and Paradise Bay are two of the greatest spots to cruise in Antarctica, where you'll view magnificent ice formations and gorgeous humpback whales. Antarctica cruises feature stops in Argentina and Uruguay, allowing you to travel across two continents in one trip.

Cruises around the United States: A transcontinental cruise, which travels between two continents, is one of the easiest and most luxurious ways to see the globe. Cruise ships travel oceans on their route to a different destination for a future cruise season, known as repositioning cruises.

Repositioning cruises are not only a terrific way to travel around the globe on a luxury cruise, but they are also frequently given at a low cost and give passengers extra days at sea to rest and enjoy all of the facilities and entertainment choices aboard.

Transatlantic sailings from Europe to North America and South America (or vice versa) and transpacific sailings from the South Pacific or Asia to North America are the two kinds of repositioning cruise itineraries available (or vice versa).

Make arrangements for a luxury cruise around the world: Now that you know how to cruise to every continent, it's time to start organizing your trip. Visit the website to learn more about our itineraries and locations, or contact one of their experienced vacation planners to help you organize an amazing journey onboard one of the award-winning cruise ships.

Chapter -17

Welcome To The Cruise

You've arrived at the port of call, and you're getting ready to board the ship and begin your holiday. What are your plans for the future? We'd like to provide a few recommendations. There's always the potential that your lodgings may be upgraded. If your ship has nicer accommodations that haven't sold yet, you may be able to negotiate a free upgrade or reduced pricing.

If the ship is cruising and the nicer accommodations are unoccupied, any money received by the cruise operator helps to reduce their losses. To check whether any are available, contact the Purser's office. For this upgrade, some cruise companies may only take cash or traveler's checks, so plan and bring plenty.

You'll most likely want to locate your cabin steward, who will be able to demonstrate how everything works. Make them your buddy; they'll come in handy. If you have your baggage, it's a good idea to unpack it so you can get it out of the way and free up some space in your cabin. If your baggage isn't in your cabin when you arrive, don't be concerned. The distribution of bags may take many hours. Inspect your cabin and report any issues right once.

However, there are a variety of different options available to you. In case of an emergency, learn how to get from your cabin to the open decks. Check to verify whether your supper seating confirmations are in your cabin; if they aren't, you should visit the Maitre d'. Check the calendar to discover when the lifeboat exercises will take place. If you want to use a spa, salon, or childcare service, locate them and sign up as soon as possible.

If you know you'll be there, look into the beach excursions. Check to see whether you can sign up right now to ensure that you get on before they sell out. Grab your deck plan and go for a stroll around the ship to get a feel for the layout and discover how to get to your stateroom from the major stairwells. Starting with the top deck and working your way down is an excellent idea. If necessary, take notes.

Every evening, you'll get a newsletter with information on the ship's activities for the next day, as well as information about supper and special events. This is something you should read every night! You won't want to miss out on anything that interests you. If you don't have time to read everything in the evening, take it with you to breakfast and read every line item. There's nothing worse than missing the "belly flop contest" or water volleyball with the crew if you're a prospective winner.

There are several activities available onboard your cruise. You'll have plenty of opportunities to eat and converse over supper. You may work off some of those calories at the ship's gym. The majority of cruise ships have fully equipped gyms, and some even provide workout courses.

You may play a game of chance at the casino or watch a movie in the ship's theater. Videos and DVDs are provided free of charge on luxury cruise ships. Because the greatest books are taken first, hurry to the library and get the ones you want. Also, be kind and return films to the library after viewing them; many passengers do not. Also, rather than purchasing a book to read on the plane, borrow one from their library.

Take enjoy some live entertainment. You'll benefit from some exceptional skills. Onboard comedians are available on many cruises to keep you entertained. Others provide dance revues in the manner of Las Vegas. Make the most of this complimentary entertainment.

The majority of cruise companies include games for passengers to enjoy. Try your luck in games like "Not So Newlywed" and "Trivial Pursuit" to win fantastic prizes! At the very least, you may win items with the cruise line's logo on them, and many of them are rather attractive. Some individuals want to be the great winners of these games because they like winning such large sums of money. Make sure you're ready for the competition.

In the lounge, you might quickly become a dancing idiot. Almost every cruise ship has a fantastic nightclub. Put your dance shoes on and get ready to boogie, boogie. Of course, full and utter relaxation is always an option. Simply relax on the balcony and soak up the sun. You deserve to relax, and what better way to do it than kicking back and relaxing on board your luxurious cruise ship?

Most cruise companies have devised a billing system for your convenience when it comes to paying for products on board. They will take a picture of your credit card and create a cruise tab for you. After your voyage, you will be given a complete cost. Keep all of the tiny receipts you sign so you can check the total at the end. This is critical since your account can be overcharged. Sign your receipts in a manner that makes them stand out and makes them tough to reproduce.

When one couple received their bill after the trip, they discovered over $600 in charges on their account for which they had no receipts. When they protested the charges and the purser looked into it, they discovered that products had been charged to their account by someone else. They would have been stuck with the surcharge if they hadn't had their receipts. The purser had no option but to erase the charges as they were.

If you don't want to spend the time after the cruise going through your bill and matching it up with your receipts, request your bill a few times during the trip and verify the receipts as you go. If you ask for a copy of your bill, they will gladly provide it, so take advantage of this and keep it on top of your bills. If the ship departs from a U.S. port, you may normally pay with a credit card, traveler's check, or U.S. dollars. If you intend on utilizing this option, you should verify the cruise line's policy on personal checks, since they are not always accepted or have restrictions.

Using your credit card instead of cash may save you money, so do so whenever possible. You'll almost certainly obtain a better exchange rate than if you changed money to spend yourself, and you'll be in a better position; credit card companies sometimes chargeback disputed expenses. When you use your credit card to buy anything, you'll often get an additional guarantee or warranty, but you should check the small print to see if there are any exclusions.

You won't have to worry about carrying and showing huge sums of cash, and if you lose your card, most credit cards have a modest maximum liability limit if you report it missing soon. It's also a good idea to use an ATM. You may minimize the danger of traveling with huge sums of cash by being able to withdraw little amounts of cash as required. Using your ATM card in a foreign country might also be an excellent method to access cash. You won't have to bother about calculating conversion rates since the ATM will give you money in local currency.

When exchanging money, use the wholesale exchange rate offered by the bank. You should still shop around to other banks since some charge a large cost for using their ATMs.

Even large ATM costs may be cheaper than what some other businesses charge for currency conversions. Don't go to an ATM until you're out of money; the machines might run out of cash or break down. We need to take a minute to discuss tipping, which is a contentious subject not just on cruise ships but also in general. As we've previously said, this is one place where you won't want to cut corners, so we'll provide some pointers.

TURN IT ON!

You'll have the chance to shop in locations you've probably never seen before while on the trip. You'll be most interested in goods that are particular to the location, such as Hawaiian coffee or Mexican maracas. Bringing gifts like this home for friends and family will ensure your popularity. Just keep in mind to budget carefully.

They'll almost certainly have snazzy stores onboard with lovely items for the low, low price of, well, you know. Prices aren't always as inexpensive as they seem! It's all too easy to be sucked into wasting time and money at the ship's onboard stores. Everything from snacks to watches to diamond jewelry is available for purchase. However, you must consider if these boutiques, with little competition, are indeed the ideal location to make luxury purchases.

It's nearly as simple to add numbers to your onboard spending by stocking up on cruise line trademark apparel, t-shirts, "designer watch sales," and "gold by the inch" instead of pricey watches and jewelry. The "in the know" passengers advise everyone to wait until the final day of the voyage when the cruise company has to get rid of its products since the cruise is almost over. At the very least, this is how many people excuse their last binge.

However, if you are one of life's unfortunates who was born with the "must shop" gene, you should wait until the final day or two of the cruise since many products are discounted at the stores aboard. Before you travel, do some research on shopping and avoid the temptation of "getting an attractive deal." When you succumb to all those lovely rings, brooches, and necklaces at the hundreds of stores on St. Thomas and elsewhere, you might soon get "clipped."

Each ship will propose particular stores (for which they will get a "kickback") and will state that they "guarantee" your purchase. This isn't immoral in the least; it's just a strategy for the cruise operator to increase money. The procedures of each cruise carrier differ, but getting your money back usually entails a nuisance (which you want to avoid on a trip, of course!). As a result, the expression "caveat emptor" applies to purchasing.

So, what does "caveat emptor" mean? The phrase means "buyer beware." Remember that putting up a duty-free sign signifies a deal to many people. There are some fantastic bargains to be obtained, but make sure you get excellent value for your money. Stick to brands you're familiar with, and make sure they're spelled correctly on the package. To put it another way, be sure it's not a forgery. Also, duty-free may simply refer to the location where you are purchasing the item. When you return to the United States, U.S. Customs has its taxes requirements.

In the United States, we see the price tag and pay it. In the Islands, however, this is not the case. If you ask for a lesser price, the seller will react with another offer. This procedure will not insult the natives or their way of life. You'll both agree on a price that is fair to both of you, and everything will be well. This can be found anywhere from the straw markets to the fancy diamond shops; a person who isn't afraid to negotiate may save a lot of money.

So keep in mind that in many parts of the globe, bargaining over the price of an item is acceptable and even expected. In the United States, guaranteed satisfaction is far more common. Make certain you understand their return and exchange procedures. Many nations do not enforce copyright rules, so the logo you see may not reflect the firm you think it does. Examine the object to discover whether it's a fake.

Some things for sale may need a specific export authorization. This is particularly true when it comes to antiques, works of art, or other culturally significant goods. Taxes may account for a much higher proportion of the buying price than in the United States. Duty-free might simply signify that the things are duty-free where they are sold. When you return to the United States, U.S. Customs has its taxes requirements.

Onboard art auctions are available on almost all cruise lines. These are major cash cows for the lines, and it's easy to be sucked into a bidding frenzy. I'd advise cruisers on a budget to avoid these auctions in general, although they're fascinating to watch. And if you really must have that Van Gogh reproduction, decide on a price range that you're ready to spend and stick to it no matter what! Another suggestion is to attend the auction on the day when complimentary champagne is provided. Another effective strategy to save money on alcoholic drinks is to do this.

When you're out shopping, keep in mind that you'll be carrying your goods home with you. It's possible that there will be limitations on what you may and cannot bring back. Check out www.customs.treas.gov/travel/know.htm, which is the Traveler Information, Know Before You Go web page of the US Treasury Department Customs Service.

This site provides information on customs declarations, duty-free exemptions, banned and restricted items, and shipping processes in the United States.

LOCATION, LOCATION, LOCATION

The many areas where the ship docks throughout your voyage are referred to as ports of call. Of course, you'll already know where the ship will dock since you thought about it before you booked. You may stretch your legs and get off the ship for a change of scenery at the ports you visit. It's vital to keep in mind that you'll just get a taste of the port or nation you'll be visiting. Most of the time (especially in the Caribbean), you will be surrounded by throngs of individuals eager to show you around the city or island or sell you something.

Some ports provide world-class possibilities to view interesting things. You'll have to determine for yourself whether or not the port is one you'd want to visit. We recommend debarking at each stop only for the experience to make the most of your vacation. You can discover that a destination that doesn't first pique your attention turns out to be one of the most fascinating places you've ever visited.

Whenever and whenever feasible, go out and immerse yourself in the local culture. You're on vacation, after all, and you want to make the most of it. The ship will provide you with activities to participate in, however, these activities are not included in your cruise package and will incur an additional price. Let's take a look at how to make the most of these beach excursions.

More Than Journeys By Bus

How can the cruiser take it all in with so many locations to see and attractions to see? Shore excursions are an important element of the cruise experience, and you should plan to participate in as many as possible. Simple sightseeing, golf, and adventure-type activities are all possible shore excursions. Decide what you want to do and join up for some exciting adventures.

Although they might be costly, you should take advantage of as many beach excursions as possible. You're on vacation, after all, and you may not get another opportunity to go parasailing, scuba diving, or whale watching! Consider a few factors while selecting the ones that are best for you. The cost of shore excursions is usually not included in the cruise fee. Shore trips might cost anything from $20 to $100 or more. Check out the various activities and sign up for the ones that interest you the most if you didn't book before boarding.

You'll want to know how much the various beach excursions cost. The majority of ship-sponsored shore excursions charge a fee. They may cost anything from $20 to many hundred dollars. You'll want to know how much shore excursions will cost ahead of time so you can compare cruise packages. The cost of shore excursions might vary significantly.

Many of the excursions offered are published on the cruise line's website, and some of them may be booked in advance before you board the ship. You should also read the information included in your ticket package. Once onboard, most cruises will provide a presentation on the port of call, as well as an overview of the various shore excursions and someone to answer any questions you may have about the packages.

To begin, get a sense of the overall game strategy to determine whether you're intrigued. Find out if you'll be coached or not; is this merely a ride or a tour? Will you be able to go on the tour while still having some spare time? On the seaside trip, how much walking or physical exercise will there be? Check to discover whether food will be given, or if you'll have to pay extra for a meal. You should also check to see whether entry and fees are included before you arrive, or if there will be additional expenses after you are there.

Regular cruisers generally agree that if you want to save money, you should schedule your trips before landing. You may book a trip in advance or hire a guide once you arrive at the dock. If you do decide to hire a tour in port, you may reduce your per-person expenses even further by sharing your guide and transportation with another couple. If you decide to do it there alone, renting a vehicle rather than hiring a cab is a good option. You'll have the flexibility to travel where you want, when you want, with a rental vehicle, and the cost may be well worth it compared to taking a taxi.

We'd like to add a word concerning taxis here. Find out ahead of time how much a taxi will cost and how long you'll have to go to get to your location. One couple I know was stranded on a Hawaiian island and wanted to go parasailing. They drove a taxi from the ship to the para-sailing area only to discover that it was whale season and they couldn't para-sail. Furthermore, the taxi ride cost them $87 for a 30-minute journey, and the only route back to the ship was via cab, which cost them another $87. It was a pricey excursion for not doing much on that particular day! Make sure your taxi driver is licensed. All of a licensed taxi driver's qualifications will be publicly displayed for all to see. HIRING AN UNLICENSED TAXI DRIVER IS NOT A GOOD IDEA. Most taxi drivers are a joy to converse with; their knowledge of the island you're visiting may be interesting; they know the best places to see, dine, gamble, and, of course, where the best beaches are.

They are also competing with one another and aim to keep their pricing cheap; remember to give them a dollar or two if their service was helpful and friendly. Onshore dining options should be discussed with the cruise director or physician. Some foods and drinks, particularly water, may be prohibited. If there are any exchange rates, be aware of them and order sensibly to optimize your budget. However, keep in mind that meals onboard are included in your cruise package, so skipping a meal and eating onboard is a fantastic way to save money.

If you go exploring on your own, you're unlikely to be protected by a ship's insurance. Before you go on a trip, make sure you know all there is to know about your ship's cruise policy. It is your responsibility to return to the departure place on time if you explore on your own. You'll have to meet the ship at the next port if you miss a launch - at your own cost. Always bring identification, the name of your ship, and the moored location with you on a beach excursion.

You should also provide a photocopy of your passport. Valuables, extra cash, and unused credit cards should all be left on board. Guides may provide you with identifying badges, but keep in mind that these badges make it easier for shopkeepers and criminals to target you. This is an excellent opportunity to discuss shore excursions and safety. As previously stated, you have the option of spending your time in the port on your own or joining a cruise line-sponsored shore excursion. Wandering a port alone may be a terrific opportunity to get away from the crowds and immerse oneself in a new culture, but it also comes with its own set of obstacles.

Because everyone for miles has been watching the enormous white ship full of visitors arrive, your prospects of fitting in undetected are slim. Even if you're traveling on a shoestring budget, the fact that you stepped off this ship qualifies you as affluent, and you are in comparison to most other regions of the globe. You must be cautious since this might put you in a risky scenario. The more information you have about a certain port and nation, the better.

A little research may go a long way toward ensuring your safety. The cruise line's shore excursions should be considered by the less experienced tourist. Although it may be more restricting than going about on your own, you may discover that you have more flexibility to enjoy seaside activities since you'll be protected. Fees for ship-sponsored shore excursions are common, so you'll want to know about them ahead of time so you can compare whole cruise packages.

To prevent becoming a victim of a pickpocket, you must pay close attention. There are a few things to bear in mind:

• Avoid traveling in tiny alleyways or dimly lit streets, and avoid being surrounded by crowds whenever possible.

• Keep your money in your front pocket and carry a fake wallet.

• Wrap your wallet in a rubber band to make it far more difficult to take out of your pocket without your knowledge.

• Keep your handbag tucked beneath your arm.

• Know the pickpocket's techniques and carry your money beneath your clothing.

Pickpockets take advantage of a variety of scenarios to free you of your valuables. When you're in one of the following scenarios, pay extra attention to your money.

- Being bumped by another person.

- Having anything spilled on you or having a stain on your clothes pointed out to you.

- A person approaching you and requesting assistance or guidance.

- Someone creating a commotion that attracts everyone's attention.

- Being in the midst of a throng, particularly if there are youngsters present.

Shore excursions are an important part of the cruise experience, so take advantage of the exotic ports you'll be visiting. Snap-in the scenery, meet the people, and take plenty of photos to share with your friends and family back home! Because you'll be spending a lot of time on the ship, let's look at some methods to save money while you're there.

FOOD, FOOD, FOOD

We must all eat! Fortunately for you, cruise ships may provide some of the most delectable and well-prepared cuisine available. You could be fortunate enough to try things you've never eaten before, and you'll want to take advantage of the delicious cuisine.

Food, food, and more food is the bargain. Breakfast, brunch, lunch, a mid-afternoon snack or tea, dinner, a midnight buffet, and room service are just a few of the dining options available. They must come up with names for all of the various meal times. You'll get up to ten chances to eat each day. Your cruise plan includes food on board, but certain extras might rapidly deplete your cash. There will be specialty coffee shops or poolside snack bars that are not included in many of the packages. Try to steer away from them if you want to save money. There's no need to add additional charges to your account for them.

Ice cream is often given for free in the late afternoon in the buffet area and as a dessert option in the dining rooms. On most ships, free coffee and tea are normally available 24 hours a day somewhere, so bring an insulated cup from home to fill up at the beverage station. You'll be able to request a certain meal hour, so it's a good idea to look into it more. With so many dining options, seating and other aspects of your cruise might be crucial.

There are two primary seating schedules on cruise ships. Breakfast is usually served about 7:00 a.m., followed by lunch at noon and supper at 6:00 p.m. Breakfast dining begins at 8:30 a.m., followed by lunch at 1:15 p.m. and supper at 8:15 p.m. These timings are not the same for every ship, but they should be close enough. Once you've decided on a mealtime, you must stick to it for the three major meals of the day. Breakfast and lunch are more flexible on certain cruises than supper.

If you are unable to make your scheduled supper, inform your waiter so that they do not have to wait for you. You'll be able to catch a variety of different meals. On a cruise ship, you can't go hungry. There are several alternative options for obtaining food. Early breakfast on the deck, maybe an informal lunch by the pool, tea, a midnight buffet, and most ships provide complimentary room service, some of which are available 24 hours a day.

It's up to you and your guests to decide which lunchtime is the best for you. Are you a night owl or a morning person? When are you most likely to dine at home? What is your favorite sort of cruise activity? The early start will limit your time on the deck for sunbathing. Your nightlife is harmed by the late sitting. If you like lingering over a lengthy meal, the later setting will feel less pressure to remove the table since there won't be another seating right after your meal.

You'll have extra time onshore to explore the ports of call or participate in shore excursions if you take the second seating. In the dining areas of many ships, there are tables for 2, 4, 6, 8, and even more people. The Cruise Line will try its best to accommodate your requests, however, like with staterooms, customers who book early have a higher chance of receiving what they want.

There are a few things to consider when determining what size table to sit at. If it's just the two of you and wants some privacy, the 2 top is the way to go. Because there are just a few two-person tables available, you'll have to move fast. For a pair, the four peaks might be perilous. You'll be sitting at a table with just one other couple, so you can get fortunate or be stuck with some duds. Many cruisers appreciate the opportunity to meet new people and prefer to sit at the bigger tables. With a larger table, you'll have a better chance of meeting people you'll like talking to.

Speak with the Maitre d' right away if you're unhappy with your sitting or your companions. They won't be able to do anything right away since all of the tables will be occupied, but they may begin working on your issue. Your seating preference should be included in the cruise information package you get after making your reservation. Some cruise lines may let you know where you will be seated before you arrive.

When you arrive, you'll normally discover a meal assignment card in your cabin. It should contain the number of your table on it. You should bring the assignment card with you to your first meal so you know where you're going. Every cruise operator will tell you that "no requests are guaranteed" and that your table assignment will be verified when you board the ship.

The worst way to start a cruise trip is to discover at the port of embarkation that the cruise company was unable to accommodate your dining preferences. For instance, you requested main seats but were allocated late seating, or you requested late seating but were given main seating. Also, if you're traveling as a couple and want a table for two, you won't know if you'll be able to get one until supper the first night. The worst-case situation is that you believe you've reserved a table for two, only to discover during dinner that you've been seated with four other couples.

To prevent these issues, make sure that your eating preferences, as well as those of everyone else in your company, are shown when you board. Your dining room assignment — early or late — and table assignment should be shown on your boarding cards supplied by the cruise company before embarkation.

Check that everyone in your party has been assigned to the same dining room and table. If not, proceed to the dining room as soon as you board the ship and speak with the Maitre d' to request the necessary alterations. If at all feasible, the Maitre d' will endeavor to meet your requests. The important thing to remember is that adjustments are done on a first-come, first-served basis, so the sooner you visit the Maitre d', the greater your chances of getting the alterations you need.

Similarly, if you plan to be seated at a table for two, go to the dining room as soon as you board the ship and locate your table (each table is numbered). If your table isn't set for two, ask the Maitre d' to modify it. Dinner is something you spend a lot of time thinking about, and you want it to live up to your expectations.

Do you want to impress your coworkers and potentially obtain better service? The majority of cruise ship staff must eat leftovers from the dining room menu or buffet (unless they want to pay for something different). You could want to inquire if they have any specific requests, and then place an order for room service and deliver it to them. (They usually want burgers!) You will earn the goodwill of these staff and get the advantages since room service is included in your registration!

Bring some Ziploc Baggies with you. They'll be quite useful on beach excursions. Order lunch from room service and put it in your Baggie to take with you to the beach. You won't have to dine at a restaurant, which will almost certainly shatter your budget. I've heard of salads costing $18.50 in Hilo, Hawaii, and tuna sandwiches costing $32 in Cozumel!

Notify the cruise company ahead of time if you have any particular dietary requirements. They will almost always be able to accommodate your specific demands. Low-calorie, low-sodium, and vegetarian options are often included on menus. However, you should still contact the lineup front to see whether your wishes may be met. As previously said, you will not go hungry while onboard a cruise ship. However, beverages may quickly deplete your cruise budget. However, there are methods to save money on them as well.

Getting Ready To Drink

Drinking on board the ship might be a costly prospect for those of you who love a swig now and again. You shouldn't expect to get plowed on $20 as you could at home. Drinks are pricey, but you can save money on them here. We'll cover both alcoholic and non-alcoholic drinks in this section.

Both may be rather costly on board, and many passengers say that this is where they spend the majority of their money, particularly if you like wine and beer. BYOB (Bring Your Beverage) is a trendy issue among cruise passengers. Many cruise companies are tolerant of passengers bringing soft drinks and bottled water on board, but they are becoming more intolerant of passengers bringing alcoholic beverages onboard. For a special event, a bottle of wine or champagne is normally OK, but don't even consider bringing a case of beer. If you have to bring your alcohol to save money, stick to soft drinks.

As you board, DO NOT take the day's umbrella drink. If you're new to cruises, you may assume this is a kind gesture on the cruise line's side. Then they ask for your stateroom number so that they may charge you $8-$9. The finest trick I've found for bringing your booze on board the cruise is about to be revealed.

LISTEN UP – THIS IS AN EXCELLENT IDEA! Send yourself a low-cost farewell present of your favorite spirits, delivered to your cabin by the cruise operator or a third-party provider. They're probably not going to put any restrictions on you having it in your cabin since it's a gift! Several websites will put them together for you for a fair price. Drinks and wine in bars are normally approximately the same price as they would be at a quality lounge or restaurant in a resort or at home (depending on where you live).

Order your umbrella drinks in standard glasses unless you want a commemorative glass to take home—you'll have to pay extra for the memento glass. At dinner, purchasing wine by the bottle saves more money than ordering wine by the glass. Any wine that you don't finish will be saved for the following evening. Wine or champagne gifts purchased from the cruise company (by you, a friend, or your travel agent) may be delivered to the dining room.

Any wine purchased elsewhere will be charged a "corkage" cost of $8-10 per bottle. If you're a beer lover, the buckets of 5 beers for $10 are a great deal. By far, this is a significant saving above the $5 per person most pubs charge.

Tap water, of course, is always ample and free. For a tasty and refreshing alternative, carry along a powdered drink mix like Crystal Light. It's simple to prepare and keep refrigerated in an insulated cup or mug, and cabin stewards keep ice buckets stocked in guest bedrooms. Alternatively, you might request a pitcher of fruit juice from room service. Juices are refreshing drinks that are also healthful.

Order the less costly "bar brand" mixed cocktails or the discounted drink-of-the-day at lounges. Every day, one will be announced in the evening bulletin. Some ships provide reduced "beverage cards" that include unlimited fountain soft drinks and/or a certain amount of mixed cocktails. Wait until you're about to set sail before purchasing these drink cards since you'll dodge the taxes and save some money!

Attend the Captain's Welcome Aboard party, when free beverages are offered and don't miss the repeaters' get-together, which is held for the same purpose. On certain evenings, art auctions typically provide free champagne, so come for the free wine and to watch people bid ridiculously high sums for terrible art.

If you like Margaritas and want something to serve in your cabin on a cruise, get the big mix bottles, tequila, and triple sec, mix them up at home, and then pour the whole concoction back into the larger mix bottle. Pack your carry-on with a double bag in Ziploc bags. A mixed drink is less likely to be seized. However, sitting about drinking in your stateroom isn't pleasant, and a huge aspect of a cruise is the sociability found in the ship's public spaces.

Keep this in mind while choosing whether or not you need alcohol in your cabin. Many ships have mini-refrigerators in the cabins. Some will let you buy soft drinks on the beach and carry them back to your cabin. Remember to bring your cup to fill up at the beverage stations. This alone will save you a lot of money on your holiday! During your trip, there will be several possibilities to engage in extracurricular activities. How can you save money while still taking advantage of what's on offer? Here are some pointers to help you get started.

Mama Is In Need Of A New Pair Of Shoes

If you're on a tight budget it's generally best to avoid the casinos onboard. They'll usually take your money and leave you with empty pockets and a bewildered expression on your face! If you like a nice game of blackjack or Texas Hold 'Em, though, you should establish a gambling limit and adhere to it at all costs. Don't spend all of your cruise money on the tables, even if you were "that close" to landing a royal flush. Make a side wager for the dealer if you must gamble.

They are rooting for you to succeed. If you have tried to put aside bet and are not as adept at Blackjack, they will be more likely to inform you when to hit or stand. Yes, you will lose at times, but that is why it is called gambling.

Sports And Other Activities

There are still methods to save money while partaking in your favorite activities while on a cruise, whether it's golf or snorkeling. If you hire snorkel gear, floats, and other water toys, the expense of a simple day at the beach may quickly escalate.

While there isn't much you can do to reduce the cost of a Jet Ski rental, you can save money by bringing your toys. Snorkeling equipment is reasonably priced at a discount and sports goods shops, and a blow-up rubber raft may be purchased for as little as a dollar. Take your own, and if you don't want to trouble to transport them home, give them away—a simple present might pleasure a local child while also saving money.

If you're going snorkeling, bring a small zip-lock bag containing corn flakes. Drop a few in the water and wait for the fish to come to you. But be careful - it has the potential to gather a large crowd! Another wonderful suggestion for snorkelers is to bring a couple of big milk-bone dog treats with you. Take one with you when you go snorkeling (easier for guys - put one in swim trunks pocket). You may rub off portions of the biscuit as it softens, and the fish will swarm. It's easier and less expensive than buying 'fish food' pills.

Scuba trips are often given for trained divers, although you may make separate arrangements with a local dive shop and bring your equipment. Don't forget to bring your underwater camera for some incredible shots! Golfers may save equipment costs by carrying their clubs, but greens fees at resort courses can be expensive. Keep in mind that you will most certainly not come across courses like those found in exotic locations.

They may be well worth the green fees, but instead of hiring a cart, try walking. Not only will you be able to work off some of the breakfast buffets, but you'll also be able to save some money while still enjoying the magnificent meals! Self-indulgence should also be a large element of any cruise trip. After all, you're on vacation! While onboard your cruise, take advantage of all that is offered to you.

Take Me Away, Calgon!

Massages, body wraps, facials, and skin treatments, as well as hair and nail services for both sexes, are available aboard modern cruise ships' comprehensive spa and salon facilities. Get haircuts and manicures before leaving home unless your cruise arrangements include this sort of treatment, and pack your paint for fingernail touch-ups.

However, if your budget permits it, we strongly advise you to treat yourself to a spa treatment. You'll not only feel better, but you'll also be calmer, allowing you to appreciate all of the activities ahead of you. We don't take the time to make ourselves feel better very often. It's the ideal time to do it while you're on vacation. Just be sure you book ahead of time. These activities are in high demand!

It's important to keep in mind that the spa staff isn't generally hired by the cruise company. They are often hired by a private firm that demands them to sell you "treatment" items at any cost. Goop worth $300 will undoubtedly reward your bank account. Even a massage may be stressful since the masseuse is marketing their products while massaging. If you really must have a Spa experience, inform your therapist that you do not want to hear any product suggestions. Maintain your composure.

You've got this! If you're one of the first onboard, you'll want to go to the spa right away. When they do the tour later in the day, you may volunteer to receive a massage or anything similar. It's free, but expect throngs of people to show up when they protest. However, since you're normally lying down on your stomach, no one can see your face! Therapy pools, steam rooms, and saunas are available on many ships. The usage of steam and sauna is usually included in the cruise cost; however, treatment pools are not always included.

Large cruise ship gyms provide a variety of complimentary fitness devices. Most basic aerobics and fitness courses are also free, however certain specialty sessions (such as yoga) and individual teaching are not. If you have any doubts, inquire about pricing before enrolling in a class. Walking and jogging around the deck are always free and are a great opportunity to get some fresh sea air.

If you want a massage, hairstyling, or other spa services on a day at sea, be among the first to board and then dash to the ship's fitness center, which is usually the first to fill. Some cruise companies, however, offer discounts on massages and spa services during the last two days of the trip. Whether a spa treatment or massage isn't at the top of your priority list, you may want to wait to see if they're on sale. You may have to have your massage while swimming in the pool, but hey, a massage is a massage! While a spa treatment or massage will undoubtedly be relaxing, many individuals find it difficult to adjust to the rocking and rolling of a ship. For some individuals, seasickness is an issue.

Oh My Painful Tummy

In general, experienced cruisers believe that the fear of seasickness is exaggerated, especially among first-time cruisers. The bigger ships have multiple stabilizers that help to smooth out the ship's pitch and roll, but in rough seas (waves of 15 feet or more), you may feel the discomfort. Many voyages nowadays take place in calm seas, and ships have become so huge that their mere bulk helps to reduce motion. By avoiding storms, modern weather monitoring technologies assist keep the ship traveling in calm seas. Large contemporary ships are becoming more technologically advanced, allowing for greater stabilizers to counteract ocean motion.

If you believe you are susceptible to seasickness, there are certain steps you may take to avoid it. Book a trip on a bigger, modern ship with stabilizers in calm conditions. Choose a stateroom on the bottom deck of the ship for the most stable journey. Choose a stateroom with beds that run parallel to the ship's length; the rocking motion is typically more comfortable for your body than the rolling motion. Spend some time on deck after you've boarded and concentrated on a specific spot on the horizon. This aids in the adjustment of your body to the movements.

Before you go, talk to your doctor about any prophylactic drugs you may be able to take. An acupressure bracelet worn around the wrists might be beneficial for certain individuals. Avoid drinking; it will only exacerbate motion sickness symptoms. You'll want to bring back memories to share with your family and friends since there are so many things to see. What is the most effective method for doing this?

NO MONEY!, NO MONEY!, NO MONEY!

Make a point of signing up for the nightly games. You won't walk away with a million bucks, but you could walk away with some great cruise line merchandise. This might range from travel mugs to canvas bags to T-shirts and other items. Some of them are very wonderful and serve as excellent mementos of your voyage. On the first day at sea, go to the "store talk." Sit at the front since they often toss out samples of products in the crowd, such as T-shirts. On one vacation, a passenger discovered a black pearl necklace in a box. A tiny bottle of vanilla and a small bottle of booze were given to another.

If you send a letter to your cruise company after your vacation, they may answer with a letter entitling you to a gift on your future voyage with them, redeemable 45 days before your next cruise. Anything from complimentary picture vouchers to a free beverage card might be included. Writing a simple thank-you note is well worth the effort. Plus, after all those years of presents, your grandmother will be delighted that you learned something!

In the casino, certain cruise companies may hand out complimentary playing cards. This might serve as a pleasant remembrance of your voyage, particularly while playing a card game with the family. As you're dealing hold 'em, rub it in. Remind everyone that you won a fantastic cruise! There is also some basic advice from seasoned sailors that will help you enjoy your vacation more.

GENERALLY

These are some basic suggestions to help you get the most out of your cruise. They were prepared based on feedback from people who had cruised on several ships and felt that these suggestions made their trip go more smoothly. Use colored post-it notes to write messages for other members of your party on the doors of cruise companions or even in your cabin. You may also leave notes for your cabin steward or housekeeping using these.

Use dollar store plastic clothespins to secure wet swimming suits and other apparel to your balcony chairs throughout the day so they don't blow away. They may also be used to hang hand-washed clothing to dry in your bathroom. Many people recommend bringing one of those inexpensive over-the-door shoe hangers as the most important thing to pack. These are the ones with pockets made of plastic.

Cruisers say they're great for keeping track of frequently used things. It is said that once you utilize it, you will understand why it is so significant. If you're a smoker, you can save money by purchasing smokes after you've boarded. You may bring your own, but if you run out, purchasing them on the ship is less expensive than buying them in port. Bring a backpack with a tote bag crammed inside with you when you go ashore.

The backpack is more convenient to transport, plus you'll have an additional bag in case you make more purchases than you anticipated. While traveling, keep all of your paperwork in a 5-pocket check holder/organizer. Label the pockets with categories like airline documents, cruise documents, cards (phone cards, insurance cards, etc.), mail, stamps, addresses, and money, where you may put all of my singles for tipping as well as traveler's checks. The benefit is that they are often wallet-sized and may be readily taken with you.

Bring baby wipes with you. They may be used for a variety of applications. If you have a stain on your clothes, use a baby wipe to remove it. It will either remove the stain or treat it in preparation for washing. Toilet paper may be scarce at ports of call restrooms. Make use of your baby wipes! They're fantastic for wiping away sticky hands and cheeks after a meal. If you're going on a cruise with friends or family, carry walkie-talkies to stay in contact. They're tiny, compact, and may save your life if you are separated on land or a large ship!

Chapter-18

How to Avoid Getting Seasick on a Cruise

If the only thing standing between you and a memorable cruise holiday on one of Celebrity Cruises' luxury ships is your fear of becoming seasick on a cruise, these motion sickness techniques will calm your mind and body, allowing you to book your trip with confidence.

This article includes the following sections:

What causes motion sickness at sea?
Seasickness is a kind of motion sickness that occurs when what your eyes perceive and what your inner ear feels are out of sync. When your body experiences motion but your eyes don't see it, your senses get confused, resulting in symptoms such as dizziness, nausea, headaches, and fatigue. Motion sickness may occur in practically every means of transportation, including vehicles, trains, and even roller coasters.

On a cruise, how long does seasickness last?
If you experience seasickness early on in a vacation, the good news is that it normally goes away as you gain your "sea legs," which means your senses adapt and your balance returns. Most guests who feel seasick at the start of a cruise will feel well in a few hours to a day or two if they take over-the-counter medications and use the procedures indicated in this article. Seasickness may linger for a long time in certain circumstances, especially when the weather is bad.

Which cruise ships are the best for avoiding seasickness?
If you're worried about getting seasick on a cruise, know that Celebrity's Solstice-class ships, which include the Celebrity Solstice, Celebrity Silhouette, Celebrity Equinox, Celebrity Eclipse, and Celebrity Reflection, are designed for smooth sailing and feature fin-like stabilizers mounted beneath the ship's waterline.

To give you a sense of how big and heavy these ships are, they're all constructed in post-Panamax proportions, which means they're too big to get through the Panama Canal's locks. They glide over the water at a pleasant average speed of 24 knots, or around 27 miles per hour, weighing between 122,000 and 126,000 tonnes. They have steel hulls and are designed with passenger safety and comfort in mind.

Celebrity's newest ship type, the Edge class, which comprises Celebrity Edge and sister ship Celebrity Apex, is the fleet's biggest. They, too, are steel-hulled vessels with stabilizers to assure the safety and comfort of the people they transport, weighing 129,500 tonnes and traveling at 22 knots, or roughly 25 miles per hour.

On a trip, where is the greatest spot to sail to prevent becoming seasick?

Avoid itineraries that spend a lot of time sailing in the open ocean if you know you're prone to motion sickness. Cruise itineraries that remain inside a sea, such as European cruises along the Mediterranean Sea or Caribbean cruises departing from San Juan, Puerto Rico, are often excellent bets for reasonably calm seas.

If you're worried about becoming seasick on a vacation, consider taking a short trip on a big ship that travels in calm waters. Celebrity Infinity, a Millennium-class ship, and Celebrity Equinox, a recently renovated Solstice-class ship, both provide 2-night trips from Florida to the Bahamas. In the normally tranquil seas between Fort Lauderdale and Miami and the Bahamas, you'll spend one day at sea in either direction. You'll have a day in port to rest and play in Nassau's bright weather, beautiful blue ocean, and white-sand beaches.

Another strategy to reduce your chances of becoming seasick on a cruise is to schedule vacation on one of the larger ships, such as the Celebrity Edge or Celebrity Apex, that sails on 10- or 11-night itineraries across the Mediterranean Sea's relatively calm waters. Cruise from Rome to some of the most picturesque places in the Mediterranean, including Sicily, Naples, and the stunning Greek Islands, on a 10-night itinerary. Sail from Rome via Naples and Messina, Corfu, Greece, and along the Dalmatian Coast to Dubrovnik and Split, Croatia, and Trieste, Northern Italy, on an 11-night itinerary.

You'll only spend two nights at sea on each of these cruises, with the rest of your time spent in port taking in the sights and sounds of the Mediterranean. Consider the time of year while planning your itinerary to minimize seasickness. For example, the optimum time to cruise the Caribbean is outside of hurricane season, which runs from June to November, since hurricanes may heighten wave height and ship movement.

On a cruise, where is the ideal cabin to prevent motion sickness?
Choose a cabin on the lowest deck in the center of the ship to avoid motion sickness. The ship's wobble will be less noticeable in this stretch. If you're afraid of seasickness on a cruise, plan a cabin with a window or a veranda, which may sound illogical. Seasickness symptoms may be alleviated with access to fresh air and a view of the horizon. If lower decks are filled or you'd prefer to be closer to the upper decks' activities, reserve a cabin in the center of the ship and avoid staterooms towards the front or rear (bow or aft). The deck layouts for the ships will assist you in determining the ideal cabin placement for your requirements.

What are the options for treating seasickness on a cruise?
Getting adequate rest on a cruise is one strategy to prevent seasickness. Motion sickness may be exacerbated by a lack of sleep or tiredness. It's essential to be prepared if you fear you'll have motion sickness on a cruise. A variety of over-the-counter, natural, and doctor-prescribed therapies are available to assist. If you opt to take a seasickness treatment, be sure to put it in your carry-on luggage and take it as instructed, which might be a few hours before boarding the ship.

Apply your transdermal patch (scopolamine) as advised by your doctor at least four hours before boarding the cruise. Because the patch is only good for three days, you should bring more if you're going on a longer trip. If you fail to bring motion sickness medicine, don't worry. Tablets to deal with seasickness may be found at the guest relations desk onboard. There are also some tried-and-true natural solutions for easing seasickness symptoms. Ginger, whether in pill or candy form, is simple to have on hand when cruising. It's also a good idea to chew on a peppermint candy or inhale peppermint oil.

Acupuncture and acupressure: Another natural technique to relieve seasickness is to wear an acupressure band around your wrist. If you want to take pressure-point treatment to the next level, skip the band and see an acupuncturist. Acupuncture technicians aboard spas might help you get rid of motion sickness.

a breath of fresh air: Though getting seasick on a cruise may make you want to cuddle up in your cabin and stay there, you'll be surprised at how much better you'll feel if you walk out and get some fresh air. At the very least, walk out onto your veranda, take a deep intake of fresh air, and keep your gaze fixed on the horizon.

Make a concerted effort to reach the upper deck and repeat the process. Inhaling fresh air while keeping your gaze fixed on the horizon might help your mind and body re-align, which may help you feel better.

What should I eat and drink on a cruise ship to prevent motion sickness?

It may seem counterintuitive, but keeping your stomach full by eating small meals and snacks throughout the day may help prevent seasickness nausea. For the first 24 hours, drinking ginger ale and eating crackers regularly may suffice. If you're prone to seasickness, limit your alcohol consumption since it might cause dehydration and worsen the symptoms of motion sickness.

It's important to stay hydrated on your vacation since dehydration might make you feel more seasick. Unlimited bottles of sparkling and still water from San Pellegrino, Acqua Panna, and Evian are included with our premium bottled water beverage plan. Browse cruise itineraries, examine cruise lodgings, fights, and activities all in one location, or chat with a cruise holiday consultant now that you know how to prevent seasickness.

Chapter-19

The Ultimate Guide to Cruising with a Toddler

Anyone who has ever traveled with a child understands how difficult it can be. After all, toddlers fidget on planes, struggle to adjust to new bedtime routines, and occasionally refuse to eat things that aren't familiar to them. You may be apprehensive to plan a cruise with a child for these reasons. Taking a child on a cruise is simpler and more enjoyable than you would think.

We wouldn't be shocked if, after sailing with your child for the first time, you decide to make a family cruise an annual ritual. Even so, there are other aspects to consider before planning your family's next cruise holiday. Here's everything you need to know about bringing a toddler on a cruise, from the finest sort of cabin to the excursions you'll want to sign up for.

This article includes the following sections:

When should a youngster be old enough to go on a cruise?
To go on most Celebrity cruises, infants must be at least six months old. Children must be at least 12 months old on transatlantic, transpacific, and select South American trips, as well as itineraries with three or more consecutive days at sea. Toddler Time (for children under the age of three) and Camp at Sea are two activities abroad designed to engage toddlers over the age of six months (ages 3 -12).

Which cruises are the greatest for toddlers?
These are some of the finest cruises to plan if you're taking your kid on his or her first trip.

Cruises departing from ports near your home city: Taking a flight before embarking on a cruise with a toddler may be stressful for both the child and the parents. By choosing a departure port near to home, you'll be able to cut down on travel time before your cruise even starts, assuring a smooth journey once you're on board. If you don't live near one of our departure ports, consider spending a day or two in the city from where you'll be sailing. This will also allow you to stock up on trip necessities including diapers, favorite foods, and sunscreen.

Cruises with a shorter duration: If this is your first cruise with a toddler, consider booking a shorter itinerary (3-4 days) to observe how your child adjusts to being on the water. If your child has previously enjoyed a cruise, go ahead and plan a longer itinerary (7-10 days), but choose one with many port calls and a few consecutive days at sea to reduce seasickness and provide more possibilities for land activities.

Cruises to places that are suitable for families: While all of our port towns provide fun and thrilling shore excursions, some are more family-oriented than others. A European city trip, for example, would not be as appealing to little children as a day spent swimming with dolphins in the Bahamas. Before choosing which cruise to take, go over the website for family-friendly activities (you can search by age).

Are cruises enjoyable for toddlers?

They are, without a doubt! Children of all ages enjoy cruises, and there are lots of activities to keep your toddlers occupied. Toddler Time takes place in the ship's playroom, where children under the age of three may play with educational items and connect with other children their age. Toddler Time requires parental supervision, but toddlers do not need to be toilet trained to engage in Toddler Time activities. You will be able to check out and return some toys and books to your cabin.

The Camp at Sea program is open to potty-trained children over the age of three. The Camp at Sea entertainment center is open daily from 9:00 a.m. to 10:00 p.m. and provides a variety of activities for kids of all ages, including STEM-focused excursions, Xbox competitions, culinary experiences, and art programs.

The Camp at Sea program also provides afternoon and sleep parties at various times of the day for parents who want a couple of hours off or maybe a romantic meal. Kids will eat a meal and participate in activities while being supervised by young staff at these events, so you can relax knowing that they will be taken care of while you have some alone time. It's a win-win scenario for all parties involved. Travelers staying in one of the suites may also make use of a choice of childcare options provided aboard.

What should I bring on a cruise with my toddler?

When on a cruise with a child, preparation is essential. We suggest carrying the following necessities in your baggage if you're going on a cruise with a toddler:

• A passport or evidence of citizenship is required.
• Snacks
• Inflatable tub
• Diapers and swim diapers
• Baby monitor
• Umbrella or folding stroller (This will come in handy since most staterooms only have a shower.)
• Sunscreen
• Children's acetaminophen, bandages, aloe gel, and antibiotic cream in a medicine/first-aid kit
• Every day, two outfits (in case there are any spills or accidents)

- One formal look (when you see the lovely images, you'll be glad you dressed your child up).
- At least three swimsuits
- Baby wipes
- Baby body wash and lotion
- Childproofing materials
- Sandals or water shoes
- Sippy cup
- Toys
- White noise machine (such as outlet plugs)

Which stateroom is ideal for families sailing with a toddler?

When taking a toddler on a cruise, the sort of cabin you pick is determined by your preferences and budget. While many cabins are suitable for families, there are certain benefits to booking a higher grade of the stateroom on your cruise if you are traveling with children.

Stateroom on the Veranda: Traveling with toddlers? Consider booking a veranda stateroom, which provides adults with a little more in-room freedom. Because children go to bed earlier, a veranda stateroom enables parents to relax on their veranda while keeping an eye on their children who are asleep inside. Even if kids have an early bedtime, you may still enjoy the view—and even a bottle of wine.

Room with a view of the ocean: Oceanview staterooms provide peace of mind and huge windows to take in the beauty outside for parents of rowdier toddlers who may choose to select a room without a balcony.

The Royal Suite is luxurious: a suite is your best choice if you want to sail in more large and unique accommodation. Suites contain not just private rooms, living spaces, and outdoor verandas, but also concierge or butler service (which may come in useful if you're having a particularly rough day with the kids), access to VIP parts of the ship, and plenty of space for busy toddlers.

On a cruise, what will my kid do?

While on a cruise, your child may participate in a variety of enjoyable activities. To begin, some of the ships include a huge outdoor pool where potty-trained children of all ages may swim, play, and splash about while aboard.

Kids may run about, play croquet, or have a picnic at the Lawn Club, a half-acre space covered with actual grass with a great view of the open sea all around. Toddler Time takes place in the ship's playroom, where children under the age of three may interact with entertaining and instructive items as well as other children their age.

Older potty-trained toddlers may also join in Celebrity Cruises' Camp at Sea program, which is available from 9:00 a.m. to 10:00 p.m. every day. Daily activities at Camp at Sea will keep the youngsters amused, including scientific trips, video game contests, art activities, and even culinary challenges. Choose from a variety of family-friendly shore excursions while in port for you and your toddler to enjoy. The options are limitless.

On a cruise, are there any babysitter services available for toddlers?

You may reserve a private babysitter on a first-come, first-served basis if you're staying in one of the suites. For $30 per hour, babysitters will look after up to three children per household. Children must be at least one year old, and each suite will be allocated up to two sitters. At least one parent or legal guardian must remain aboard the ship if you want in-suite babysitting on a port day. Children in the youth program, aged 3 to 12, may attend the ship's afternoon parties (from 12:00 pm to 2:00 pm and 5:00 pm to 7:00 pm) and sleep parties (from 10:00 pm to 1:00 am), where they will be monitored by personnel.

On a cruise, what will my kid eat?

Parents of finicky eaters may be concerned about what to feed their toddlers aboard a cruise ship. Fortunately, cruises make it simple. Toddlers may order from the kid's menu in the main dining area, which offers classics such as spaghetti bolognese, grilled cheese sandwiches, tiny margarita pizzas, and cheeseburgers with fries.

If your youngster is too weary to have a sit-down dinner, they also provide an in-room dining menu with chicken skewers with yogurt sauce, hot dogs with fries, and a range of desserts. For parents sailing with toddlers, a buffet is a fantastic choice. There's a wide variety of meals to choose from, and the atmosphere is more informal and easygoing. In addition, the buffet includes an ice cream and dessert bar, which is guaranteed to please any child.

Is it necessary for me to carry a stroller?
To travel from one place to the next aboard a cruise ship, you may have to walk a long distance. Bring a stroller on board to make things simpler for your young one (and your back). It's recommended that you leave the cumbersome stroller at home and carry a lightweight umbrella stroller that folds up small enough to fit under your bed or in your stateroom's closet. If you don't want to carry a stroller, a baby wrap or baby carrier that can comfortably hold your toddler would do. Strollers and carriers are very useful in port, especially if you intend on doing some shopping or strolling between the cruise ship and the town.

What kinds of beach excursions am I allowed to do with my toddler?
A family-friendly shore excursion offers an enjoyable, hassle-free day in port when you have a toddler. We provide a variety of family-friendly shore excursions that everyone in your group will love. If you're traveling with a child, look for a beach trip that doesn't have an age limit.

Also, bear in mind that an excursion that demands a lot of sitting (such as lengthy bus journeys in port) may not be the finest or most convenient activity for your kid. Instead, seek excursions that include short, simple treks or an activity they'll like, such as gold panning on Alaska cruises or a Caribbean water park trip.

Chapter-20

What is Accessible Travel for Seniors with Disabilities?

According to the World Health Organization (WHO), around 15% of the world's population is disabled. With 7.5 billion individuals on the earth, around one billion have a disability. That is why, now more than ever, it is critical for globe travel to be accessible to everyone. The accessible travel movement is a call to action to make global travel more accessible, safe, and enjoyable for persons with physical disabilities, those who use wheelchairs, those who have health issues, and those who have special needs.

Finding information about accessible travel is an important component of preparing for people with disabilities and others who accompany them. Finding useful information in one location might be tough. You'll discover useful connections to access resources, destination-specific ideas, and other methods for people with disabilities to advocate for themselves and others when traveling in this guide.

The World Tourism Organization (UNWTO) acknowledges particular conditions for ethically accessible tourism on a global scale, and sites may even be designated as "Accessible Tourism Destinations." The Americans With Disabilities Act, signed into law in 1990, specifies particular accommodations and outlaws discrimination against people with disabilities in the United States. Cities around the United States, especially urban regions, have undertaken the lengthy and difficult process of enormous infrastructure upgrades to make their cities more accessible, such as the Metropolitan Transportation Authority of New York City (MTA).

According to Curbed NY, just 117 of the 472 MTA subway stations in New York City are accessible. Curbed also has a map of the stations that are wheelchair accessible. Our goal is to raise awareness regarding travel accessibility so that the world's destinations may continue to improve. Whether you're just starting your holiday planning or ready to leave, use this guide as a starting point for your study.

While this may not cover all there is to know about accessible travel and travelers' rights, putting information on accessible travel in one place is a modest step toward making the traveler's trip less about scouring the Internet for information and more about enjoying the adventure. Travelers with disabilities may also use blogs, forums, and message boards to gather information about accessible attractions, lodgings, and itineraries. Before you start looking for accessible travel destinations, consider the following tips. When traveling with a handicap, such as impaired eyesight or in a wheelchair, you may need to do more research to ensure that you can navigate without stress and worry.

Using the services of a travel agency or a licensed accessible travel concierge to assist you to organize the details on the ground may be beneficial, as they can research accessible activities and design your schedule for you. Accessible travel packages and destination information are often available from travel agencies, especially those managed and assembled by travelers with mobility limits and impairments. A couple that travels often despite dealing with a motor accident runs the blog Accessible Getaways. accessible contains information about accessible sites and locations all across the United States and can help you search by destination.

Once you've selected where you want to travel, visiting the websites of potential locations may frequently provide valuable planning advice. In places like Florida, there's even a list of accessible itineraries and services, ranging from wheelchair rental providers to accessible beaches. Cruises are also a viable alternative for tourists who prefer to have their itinerary selections made for them rather than depending on their research since cruise ships are obliged by law to comply with specific ADA compliance rules. With accessible travel, it's best to focus on one or two places that have a plethora of information available rather than a whole nation or continent. This is only a small example of the places you may see if you want to plan your trip.

In the United States, museums are required by law to meet specific museum access criteria under the American With Disabilities Act (ADA), thus if you're looking for things to do on vacation, museums are likely to be more accessible than other options. For further information about accessibility options, call ahead or check the website of the exact museum you're interested in visiting, such as the Museum of Modern Art in New York City or The Smithsonian in Washington, D.C. Some blogs promote New York museums that are accessible to those with poor vision.

If you're planning a trip outside of the United States, Pantou, which derives its name from the Greek word for "everywhere," provides a comprehensive list of accessible European locations and services for people with all sorts of impairments.

Information to Bring With You Checklist
If you're going on a trip, you'll almost certainly have a comprehensive packing list. The same is true for disabled tourists and their caregivers. Whether you're going by land, sea, or air, be sure you have these essentials with you.

1.Bring all necessary paperwork and medical information, including any allergies.

2. You must have valid identification and a passport everywhere you travel.

3. Bring prescriptions in your carry-on rather than your checked baggage, and make sure they're all properly labeled to make traveling simpler, whether it's passing through airport security or settling into your hotel room.

4. If you or someone you're traveling with takes prescription drugs, have a note of all the pills you're taking, the time you take them, and any other health-related instructions handy in case of an emergency. Just in case, bring extra dosages of all medications.

5. If you have a service dog, make sure you bring up-to-date vaccination information, treats, and food with you on any lengthy excursions to ensure your service dog is comfortable.

6. If you have a mobility handicap or use a wheelchair, you may wish to carry a portable battery or spare components with you just in case. This will depend on the sort of mobility assistance you need and your preferences.

Your Legal Rights:
There are some rights you have as a traveler that are supposed to safeguard you, according to the Americans With Disabilities Act and other anti-discrimination legislation across the world. This informative article from Smarter Travel explains your rights as a disabled passenger while flying.

Even while airlines and hotels are coming up to the demands of their passengers, traveling with a handicap may be difficult; things like bed heights, shower knobs within reach inside hotel rooms, and air travel bathrooms are still not optimized for people with disabilities. This may be disappointing and cause anger between passengers and travel suppliers.

Accessible Cruising is a great way to get there

Another alternative for travelers with impairments and their carers is to take a cruise holiday. Special needs cruises and accessible cruises have made significant progress in providing accessible cabins on cruise ships, incorporating bars and rails, Braille signs for individuals with visual impairments, and additional help while boarding and disembarking. The National Association of the Deaf also has guidelines for cruise companies to follow to make them accessible to deaf passengers.

Some cruise ships even accept service animals onboard, depending on rules. During the cruise planning phase, it is strongly advised that you contact a customer care professional to tailor your cruise experience and accommodations. Some cruise companies urge passengers to fill out a special needs form so that their particular requirements are satisfied and expectations are surpassed while on board.

Popular travel websites like Fodors provide advice on cruise ships for disabled passengers, including planning ideas. Special Needs at Sea has a collection of links to various cruise lines as well as information on cruise accessibility.

Wheelchair-Friendly Travel Resources

Traveling with a wheelchair has unique problems, and it may be stressful to determine whether your destination, restaurant, or activity will have wheelchair ramps and other accessible facilities. Information regarding wheelchair-friendly travel is rapidly rising each year, whether you're preparing for your trip or planning to join an accessible cruise.

Some sites, such as Scootaround, even offer particular wheelchair-friendly places around the globe to bear in mind during the vacation planning phase(https://scootaround.com/en/13-of-the-most-wheelchair-accessible-travel-destinations).

Wheelchair Traveling (https://wheelchairtraveling.com/) provides basic information about traveling with a wheelchair.

Autism and Traveling

Because autism is a spectrum disorder that varies from person to person, a person with autism has special requirements while traveling. Some autistic persons are very sensitive to noise and need a quiet atmosphere. Others may find lengthy travel days tiring, therefore low-impact activities should be planned. Large crowds, lengthy queues, and abrupt schedule changes may be distressing to those with autism.

- Autism Speaks (https://www.autismspeaks.org/) is a website dedicated to providing broad information about the condition.

- Autism Travel (https://autismtravel.com/) has a travel directory of Certified Autism Centers, as well as information, resources, and a travel directory.

- The National Autism Association (https://nationalautismassociation.org/) also offers educational programs and information about autism, as well as support for families and the newest breakthroughs in diagnosis.

- Autism on the Seas (https://autismontheseas.com/) is a vacation resource developed in partnership with Royal Caribbean that offers staff-assisted holiday cruise packages to people with autism and their families.

- The Society for Accessible Travel and Hospitality has compiled a list of 10 must-know guidelines for traveling with autism, including a list of must-have goods for your trip, techniques for caregivers to prepare travelers with autism for their experiences, and more.

Whether they have poor vision or their hearing has been compromised by aging, millions of individuals throughout the globe are afflicted by hearing and vision issues. There are several tools available to assist travelers with hearing or visual impairments. The National Association for the Deaf (https://www.nad.org/resources/transportation-and-travel/) provides basic information regarding transportation and travel while deaf for individuals who are deaf or need a hearing aid.

The Christopher Reeve Foundation provides a series of films about accessible travel, including hiring a vehicle, air travel, hotels, and more, for people with disabilities who like video. (https://www.christopherreeve.org/living-with-paralysis/home-travel/video-accessible-travel) Hearing-impaired people may also get closed captioning.

More Apps and Online Resources
• Lonely Planet message boards for disabled travelers. (https://www.lonelyplanet.com/landing/lonely-planet-community) As you plan your trip, a feeling of community may be a useful tool for asking questions, engaging with other travelers, and learning more about accessible places.

• The Accessible Travel Forum (https://www.tabifolk.com/) provides forums, guides, and community debates concerning destination accessibility on all seven continents.

• Be My Eyes (https://www.bemyeyes.com/) is an app that links a blind or low-vision individual with a competent volunteer through video conference to give virtual help, such as navigation or grocery shopping. Both iOS and Android versions are available.

• Navability (https://briometrix.com/navability/): For individuals traveling in a wheelchair, the in-development (https://briometrix.com/navability/) Navability will assist you in geolocating yourself and calculating the optimum route for a wheelchair user.

• ATM Finder (https://www.link.co.uk/consumers/locator/) If you're visiting the United Kingdom, you may use this handy list of ATM locations.

Everything You Need to Know About Cruises for Seniors with Disabilities

Onboard, on easy-to-navigate cruise ships, you'll discover tastefully equipped accessible bedrooms and public places. All passengers may participate in a variety of onboard activities, including trivia contests and wine matching workshops, as well as destination briefings, exhilarating entertainment, and quiet meditations. Seniors with impairments will also get help from ship to shore, making the boarding process as simple and pleasant as possible.

Ships that are easily accessible

Accessible features are available on all Celebrity cruises, allowing seniors with disabilities to navigate about the ship and enjoy all of the activities and services available. On Solstice-class and Edge-series ships, large hallways that can accommodate wheelchairs and power scooters, conveniently situated elevators, and power doors may be found throughout the ship. All dining, bar, and lounge locations, as well as aboard theaters, provide accessible seating.

Public places, including public restrooms, have open and pleasant environments with moderate inclines for easy access. Play games at reduced tables and slot machines at the onboard casino. A chair lift will assist you in entering the pool or hot tub when you're ready to relax in the sun. In addition to Braille signs in elevators and public spaces, Celebrity Today, a daily newsletter, is provided in both Braille and big type. Menus in large print are also accessible at all dining establishments.

You'll get assistance with transportation from the airport to the pier, boarding, and exiting the ship for cruise excursions to guarantee that your cruise experience is excellent from beginning to finish.

Staterooms with Wheelchair Access

Accessible cabins are available on all of the premium cruise ships, and each has been carefully created for disabled passengers. Wider doors with reduced door sills, for example, make it easier for wheelchair and power scooter users to go in and out of accessible staterooms. Our accessible veranda cabins include wheelchair-accessible balconies so you can enjoy the view. Select staterooms have a five-foot turning radius for simple mobility.

Guests with specific requirements for sight or hearing may request an accessible stateroom. Onboard, there are teletypewriters (TTY), portable room kits with a visual-tactile warning system for door knocking, telephone ringing, alarm clocks, and smoke detectors. Closed captioning is available on all televisions in the staterooms.

Inaccessible rooms must have additional features such as lowered closet clothes bars, a roll-in shower with handheld showerheads, grab bars, and a fold-down shower bench, as well as lower basins and vanities, taller toilets, and ramped thresholds in the bathroom. Staterooms with handicapped access are conveniently positioned near elevators.

Before you book your vacation, go through the ship's deck plans to determine where the public spaces are situated and choose the one that is closest to them. Accessible cabins are reserved for disabled passengers until all non-accessible accommodations in that category are sold out. Because there are only a few accessible accommodations on board, it's best to book early and fill out the requisite special needs form, or to book with one of the holiday consultants.

Assistance with Medical Issues

A clinic with a doctor and two nurses is available 24 hours a day aboard all Celebrity cruises. Basic drugs, such as seasickness medicine, aspirin, and other common cures, are available in the ship's pharmacy. Because the onboard pharmacy is unable to fill prescriptions, bring a sufficient quantity of your medicine with you and store it in your carry-on baggage so you can access it as soon as you board. You may also travel directly to your cabin with Celebrity Cruises Open Access before visiting the ship.

Dialysis

Onboard, there are dialysis stations, although only ambulatory peritoneal dialysis may be performed. Celebrity Cruises is unable to provide hemodialysis or help with dialysis treatments while on board. Guests who need peritoneal dialysis should have the necessary solutions and equipment supplied to the ship at least two hours before embarkation day. Please contact us for additional information about our dialysis rules and procedures on board.

Oxygen

Onboard, oxygen cylinders are permitted. Before boarding, passengers must communicate the kind of oxygen cylinder, amount, and delivery schedule. Because our regulations vary based on the ship, please contact us for further information on the oxygen storage needs of each ship.

You'll sail to your destination on one of the luxury ships with fully-equipped and thoughtfully designed accessible features for seniors with disabilities, whether you're admiring the green hills of Ireland, getting up close and personal with koalas and kangaroos down under in Australia, seeing the magnificent mountains and glaciers of Alaska, exploring the temples of busy Hong Kong, or unwinding on the white-sand beaches of a sunny Caribbean Island.

You may arrange shore excursions that are tailored to your interests and activity level at each port stop on your cruise itinerary. Consider private travels, which are highly customized excursions, small group tours, or destination tours that transport you in a wheelchair-accessible van to the city's most prominent sites and attractions.

Chapter-21

Everything You Need to Know About Getting Married at Sea

It's no surprise that so many couples prefer to marry at sea. With the boundless ocean as a background, exotic port destinations, and a built-in honeymoon, it's no surprise that so many couples choose to marry at sea. If you've just been engaged (congrats!) and are considering having your wedding on a cruise, there are a few things to consider before saying "I do."

Here's everything you need to know about getting married at sea, whether you're planning a destination wedding in an international port or a small ceremony aboard with just a few guests.

This article includes the following sections:

Is getting married on a cruise ship legal?
To ensure that your aboard or onshore wedding is legally binding, you must first get a marriage license. You'll obtain an official marriage certificate after being married aboard a cruise ship, which you may use as legal evidence of your marriage.

Is it legal to marry aboard a ship in international waters?
Some couples choose to marry at one of the port cities, but if you want to consider being married on a Celebrity Cruises ship while cruising in international seas, you'll need to secure a marriage license from Malta. Why did you choose Malta? A wedding ceremony at sea must be done in accordance with the regulations of the nation in which the ship is registered, and all Celebrity Cruises ships are registered in Malta. As a result, if you want to marry at sea, our staff will gladly help you in obtaining a license from Malta during the planning stage of your wedding.

What is the cost of getting married on a cruise ship?

The cost of getting married on a cruise ship varies based on the port place where you want to marry. You may check all of the wedding port alternatives on the Celebrity Weddings and Events website and get critical information like projected price (for both shipboard and on land weddings), marriage license requirements, and venue options. Getting married abroad provides all of the advantages of a destination wedding with none of the drawbacks.

The majority of wedding and event packages include necessities like an indoor or outdoor ceremony site, a reserved interior reception room with food and beverage service, flower arrangements for the couple, cake and champagne, and a photographer. Once you've decided on the kind of wedding you want, event planners will assist you in selecting the proper venue and package based on what's most important to you and your partner, ensuring that your cruise wedding is a stress-free experience.

Is it possible to marry a ship's captain at sea?

In the United States, most cruise ship wedding ceremonies are conducted by a notary public, and in overseas ports, by a non-denominational officiant. If you want your wedding to be administered by a ship's captain, you'll have to marry while traveling on international seas. The rules of the nation where the ship is registered are followed during ceremonies at sea administered by the ship's captain. You must first get a Maltese wedding license before getting married at sea aboard a Celebrity Cruises ship.

Also, if you're being married at sea by a ship's captain, your wedding ceremony cannot take place on embarkation day or night and must take place between 10:00 a.m. and 2:00 p.m. in order for the ship's crew to complete their jobs effectively.

On a ship, how do you organize a wedding?

Celebrity Cruises can organize your wedding for you if you opt to be married on a cruise. To begin, go to the Weddings and Events website and familiarize yourself with the many wedding and event packages we have available.

Then, before making a decision, investigate potential wedding ports and compare factors such as cost and marriage license requirements. Once you've decided on your wedding location, look for available dates and times, submit a request form, and one of our event managers will contact you to begin the wedding planning process. Then, until embarkation day, you and your spouse can sit back and relax while Celebrity Cruises handles all the logistics.

Are our wedding planners available on cruise ships?

Event Managers and Wedding Coordinators will be available to couples getting married aboard a Cruises ship. Before boarding your cruise, Event Managers assist you with all of the necessary planning. They'll answer any questions you have, help you narrow down your venue options, aid with reservations, and get the right paperwork for your ceremony, among other things.

Wedding Coordinators will be your point of contact during your cruise and will assist you in planning your wedding day to ensure that everything runs well.

What is the greatest cruise ship for a wedding?

What you want for your wedding ceremony and reception will determine which cruise is ideal for you. Whether you want to marry in Italy while on a European cruise or be married on board with the captain as your officiant, we have lots of amazing experiences and over 200 places to choose from.

Choose a romantic cruise that includes a stop in one or more honeymoon sites like Hawaii, the Bahamas, or the French Riviera. Wine tastings, award-winning plays, and quiet lunches in the Lawn Club await you and your loved one on board. Is it necessary for my guests to be on a cruise to attend my wedding?

Even if they aren't passengers, guests may join a cruise ship and celebrate your wedding with you on specific dates. Your wedding ceremony and reception must take place at one of the embarkation ports on a sailing day in order for non-sailing guests to be able to join festivities aboard.

That said, part of the enjoyment of having a cruise wedding is being able to experience all of the benefits of traveling with Cruises with you and your wedding guests. Not only can you hold your wedding aboard or at one of the numerous port locations, but your family and guests will be able to enjoy excellent cuisine, kid-friendly activities, and world-class entertainment while onboard. For everyone, it's the ultimate stress-free, all-inclusive wedding experience.

Is it possible to have a same-sex marriage at sea?
While in international seas, cruise captains may perform legally recognized same-sex marriages. When you marry while traveling on international seas, the wedding is conducted according to the rules of the country in which the ship is registered. Because same-sex weddings were made legal in Malta in 2017, same-sex couples may now marry aboard Celebrity Cruises while at sea. In nations where same-sex weddings are allowed, they may also take place on land.

What should I do if I want to propose on a cruise?
Celebrity Cruises also provides proposal packages to help you pop the question at the most inopportune time if you're searching for a unique and unforgettable method to ask someone to marry you.

Reserving a secluded table for two in one of our specialty restaurants onboard, securing a photographer to be on hand and take engagement photos right after your partner says yes, decorating a stateroom with sparkling wine and chocolate-covered strawberries, and sending a gourmet breakfast in bed the morning after the proposal are all included in our proposal packages.

You may also hire an Event Manager or Event Coordinator to work with you before and during the cruise to ensure that everything is in place for your proposal. Are you ready to start planning your ideal wedding or proposal from the comfort of your own home? Visit the website's Weddings page to learn more about Cruises' wedding packages and locations.

Chapter-22

The Ultimate Honeymoon Cruise Planning Guide

Honeymoon cruises are the perfect antidote to the flurry of activity that goes along with wedding preparation and celebrations. It requires some forethought to ensure that it fulfills its intended aim of allowing you to breathe, relax, reconnect, and enjoy your first shared experience as a married couple. Here's how you arrange the ideal honeymoon cruise, step by step. Learn how to choose the ideal itinerary and make your onboard experience as romantic as possible.

This article includes the following sections:

Choose the Ideal Vacation Spot

Do you want a romantic Caribbean trip where you may relax on a white sand beach while admiring the turquoise waters? Have you ever wished to visit the Eiffel Tower, the Tower of London, or the Rock of Gibraltar's high cliffs? Are you looking for an amazing trip to a faraway location that you can tell your grandchildren about?

The greatest honeymoon cruises take you to places that match your interests, personality, and level of activity. Consider how you want to spend your time together, whether it's seeing European cities, relaxing on side-by-side chaises on a sunny beach, or trekking in the Caribbean.

Honeymoon cruises to the Caribbean feature activities like sunbathing or strolling on gorgeous white-sand beaches, snorkeling coral reefs with colorful tropical fish, sailing on a catamaran at sunset, ziplining over a jungle, and parasailing over the sea. A romantic holiday to the Mediterranean that mixes discoveries of food and wine with local culture, art, and history will satisfy your inner gourmet.

In the Italian countryside, sip local wine, experience tapas in Spain, and fill up on fresh seafood along Europe's coastline. Explore historical sights and landmarks while admiring works made by the world's greatest recognized painters. Some of the greatest cultural cruises you'll ever take are in the Mediterranean.

Consider Asia cruises to Japan, with its calm beauty, or Vietnam and Thailand, which are bursting with people and bustle, if you both like exotic locales. You'll spend many days at sea on these itineraries, making use of your ship's opulent facilities. Couples massages, adult-only pools, and hot tubs, and romantic meals in onboard specialty restaurants with world-class cuisine are just a few of the amenities available. It's your time to travel the globe together, so whichever route you take will be unforgettable.

Choose a Stateroom

Nothing beats slipping into soft bedding after an exciting day in port, toasting to your new life together on your own terrace, and waking up to breathtaking ocean vistas on a honeymoon cruise. After you've decided on your cruise itinerary, the following step is to pick your cabin or suite. A veranda suite with beautiful sea and sky views will undoubtedly make for a wonderful honeymoon cruise, but why not surprise each other with an upgrade that will make your vacation even more spectacular?

Our AquaClass cabins, which include spa-inspired in-room amenities, unrestricted access to the SEA Thermal Suite or the Persian Gardens (depending on which ship you fly on), and free dining at Blu, are ideal for spa fans. Book The Retreat for a holiday unlike any other, which includes a magnificently furnished room, the services of a Personal Retreat Host, priority embarkation and disembarkation, exclusive access to Luminae, and access to a special lounge exclusively for Retreat guests.

Reservations are required

When you were investigating your cruise itinerary, did you come across any intriguing shore excursions? Perhaps it was a trip to a waterfall on Hawaii's main island, a Caribbean horseback ride, and swim, or a pasta-making session at a Tuscan villa. Then there are the ship's romantic amenities, such as couples massages and supper at one of the ship's specialty restaurants.

You'll establish an account when you book your cabin, and from there you'll be able to book shore excursions, specialty restaurant dining reservations, and spa treatments. Make those unique reservations now, rather than waiting until you're on board the ship after you've booked your vacation.

The most popular shore excursions, as well as specialized restaurants and spa appointments, might sell out months in advance of the cruise's departure date. You'll be able to relax and enjoy your time on the ship (and with each other) without the stress of searching for last-minute bookings if you book early.

Boost the Romance

Romantic parties are defined by wine, flowers, and chocolate-dipped strawberries. Begin your honeymoon cruise with a Celebrity Cruises Celebration Package that will surprise and delight your true love and carry on the romance and celebration of your wedding. The Classic Celebration Package includes a bottle of La Crema Pinot Noir, a beautifully arranged arrangement of flowers, and a dozen plump and scrumptious chocolate-dipped strawberries.

When you pick the Deluxe Celebration Package, your stateroom will be supplied with Dom Perignon Champagne and mimosas for a nice romantic breakfast, as well as a bouquet of fresh flowers and those luscious chocolate-covered strawberries. A customized cake is also provided as a nice treat to savor later in the day.

The romantic extras you may organize on your honeymoon cruise aren't limited to special stateroom delivery. Celebrity's Private Journeys are unique shore excursions that let you arrange your ideal day in port. You'll get access to a Destination Insider staff member who can help you plan your special day down to the last detail, including your own vehicle and driver, helicopter flights, and private excursions - or anything else you have in mind.

Investigate the Ship

Every evening on a cruise ship, there is so much to do that you can treat every night like a date night. Take in a Broadway-worthy production in the theater after an outstanding supper at one of the specialty restaurants, then walk to one of the bars to dance to DJ spins or listen to live music while sipping a hand-crafted cruise drink.

Try something unusual and entertaining that you haven't done before, such as karaoke, bingo, or trivia games. Combining a Honeymoon Cruise with a Wedding at Sea is a great way to spend your honeymoon. The ideal honeymoon cruise may simply begin with a wedding at sea for couples who like traveling.

Nothing is more convenient or romantic than being married on a ship and then sailing away on your honeymoon. Celebrity Cruises provides every kind of wedding planning service possible, including a pre-inspection package that allows couples and their guests to tour the ship's wedding and reception facilities, discuss wedding arrangements, and enjoy a buffet lunch.

Exchanging vows at sea while the ship is in international waters; shipboard weddings where vows can be exchanged in port before sailing away on a honeymoon; shoreside ceremonies in over 200 destinations around the world; and onboard reception-only celebrations are all available as cruise wedding packages.

You'll have the support and help of a professional event manager who will oversee all of the shipboard wedding arrangements, from flowers to food to music to bridal party make-up, to ensure everything is flawless. You'll also have an event organizer who can help you with things like canopies, seats, and canapes in the port.

Your ship's captain is licensed to officiate your wedding ceremony on board, and if you're being married in port, your wedding organizer may arrange for an officiant.

Chapter-23

From Florida, these are the top five Thanksgiving cruises.

Thanksgiving cruises from Florida are the ideal cure to the stresses of feeding, lodging, and entertaining relatives throughout the holiday season. Take a Thanksgiving cruise trip on one of the finest cruise ships visiting some of the Caribbean's most sought spots.

Enjoy a stress-free Thanksgiving meal aboard your Celebrity ship, complete with a traditional turkey dinner and all the fixings. At the casino bar, you may watch the big game and participate in family-friendly themed game shows. Aside from the food, your cruise holiday will include relaxing on gorgeous beaches, seeing intriguing marine life, and participating in exciting shore excursions. Some of the greatest Thanksgiving cruises departing from Florida are listed here.

This article includes the following sections:

From Tampa, go to the Caribbean and the Americas
On an 11-night Thanksgiving trip from Florida, unlock the ultimate Caribbean cruise experience and explore some of the greatest of the Americas. The secluded island of Grand Cayman is your first destination after a fantastic day at sea. Swim inside a buried World War II naval vessel for an unusual and unique viewpoint (and amazing photos), then wander down Seven Mile Beach on Grand Cayman.

Immerse your senses in the ideal combination of colonial and Colombian charm in Cartagena. Take a tour of the ancient Getsemani district, a walled-off walking region that has been culturally (and mainly architecturally) maintained for centuries. Take a day excursion to the Magic Mud Volcano or go swimming in the adjacent Islas de Rosario archipelago to learn more about the local environment.

As you sail to Colon aboard the Celebrity Constellation, you'll arrive at the entrance of the world-famous Panama Canal. Visit the stronghold of Portobelo and Gatun Lake, as well as the Caribbean coast of Panama. Visit the Ancon Hill urban jungle or browse in the stores along Casco Viejo's cobblestone streets on a day trip to Panama City. Finish your trip with a fun and instructive day at the Panama Canal Museum for the whole family.

On the eighth day of your luxurious Caribbean vacation, take a cruise to Costa Rica. With unmatched access to the country's rainforests and animal reserves, you can experience nature protection and preservation at its finest in Puerto Limon. Get up and personal with Costa Rica's 850 distinct bird species, as well as the 500,000 other animal species that call the country home. As you buy and prepare to return to the sea, tempt your taste buds with organic tropical fruits at the lovely port area.

End your journey on the Mexican island of Cozumel, a historic Mayan colony that harmoniously mixes indigenous heritage and current Caribbean culture. Take a tequila lesson and learn how to make margaritas. Then eat fresh fish grilled with exquisite Mexican spices and tastes while shopping for handcrafted gifts made from rare minerals. As the sun sets behind you, end the day with a homemade drink on a white sand beach with a background of Mayan artifacts.

From Fort Lauderdale, go to the Panama Canal and the Southern Caribbean

On this incredible 11-day trip through the Panama Canal and the exquisite Southern Caribbean, paradise awaits. Aruba is the ideal first stop on this Thanksgiving cruise from Florida, with fantastic beaches, shopping, eating, and family-friendly activities.

Take a leisurely stroll around Pelican Pier, where you may eat fresh seafood while admiring the scenery. On a water slide or a speed boat trip around De Palm Island, splash about and let your daring side run wild. Curaçao, another Dutch colonial treasure in the Southern Caribbean, is your next visit to the Netherlands Antilles. In Willemstad's old city, near the harbor, you'll discover world-class shopping and restaurants. Learn about the island's history and how it grew into what it is now at the UNESCO-protected 17th-century Fort Amsterdam. Curaçao is a melting pot of cultures, colors, and tropical pleasure in one place.

Then fly to Bonaire, where you'll find world-class diving and untouched beauty at every turn. Delight your senses with a tour of Kralendijk's Dutch-inspired stucco houses, then try your luck at the one-of-a-kind barefoot casino. Try "Yambo," a typical Creole soup, at one of Bonaire's Rincon district's numerous real gourmet restaurants.

Colon, near the entrance of the Panama Canal, is the gateway to the Americas. Here you'll discover vestiges of Panama's history mixed together with the enormous canal's current technological wonder. Visit Portobelo's fortress and ruins, or relax on Isla Grande's beautiful white-sand beaches. Then go along the Panama Canal's locks, a world marvel that has transformed global trade and economy.

End your fantastic Thanksgiving cruise at the historic city of Cartagena, Colombia. Enjoy the diverse food scene, shopping, and physical history that you will encounter at every step. Thrill-seekers may try kitesurfing, which is one of the area's primary sporting attractions or take a day excursion to the nearby Magic Mud Volcano.

From Miami, go to Key West and the Bahamas

The gorgeous Bahamas beaches and charming Key West make for an ideal four-day Thanksgiving cruise from Miami. Leisure is a way of life in Key West, and you'll notice it the moment you arrive.

This legendary island has more (and better) bars and restaurants per square foot than anyplace else on the planet. Take a boat cruise to see dolphins or snorkel over coral reefs. At the Key West Butterfly and Nature Conservatory, you can learn about unusual native flora and wildlife. End your day with a visit to Dry Tortugas National Park's stronghold, which is the biggest brick edifice on the east coast.

Nassau, Bahamas' busy seaport, is the country's cultural capital and an excellent destination for boutique shopping, museums, and cuisine. Take a short boat ride to the Blue Lagoon for a private, uncrowded beach experience.

The Nassau Straw Market has hand-woven purses, caps, and other artisan goods. Snorkel along the beach to see sea turtles in their natural environment. Finish your trip to Nassau with live music and a margarita on Bay Street, just steps from the Atlantis resort. Puerto Rico, Tortola, and St. Kitts are the fourth and fifth places on the list. From Fort Lauderdale, take a cruise. For a luxurious Thanksgiving cruise from Florida that your family will never forget, sail for seven nights aboard the groundbreaking Celebrity Apex.

Spend a day at sea experiencing the ship that raises the bar on luxury and service. Staying at The Retreat gives you unique access to The Retreat Sundeck, The Retreat Lounge, and Luminae, so you can make the most of your vacation. Puerto Rico's pristine beaches are backed by lush foliage and jagged mountains. Admire the spectacular views from the 500-year-old fort of Old San Juan. Visit the Museo of Arte de Puerto Rico or have a spectacular Bacardi Rum tour with adult family members.

Visit the Virgin Islands Fold museum in Tortola to learn about the fascinating history of the magnificent island chain. Hike one of Sage Mountain National Park's numerous challenging paths for the greatest vistas and mild coastal breezes. Train rides through St. Kitts provide spectacular views of a dormant volcano. Alternatively, take a boat from one island to the next and relax on one of Nevis' beautiful beaches.

Bahamas, Mexico, and Grand Cayman are the top five. From Fort Lauderdale, take a cruise.

Enjoy a seven-night cruise to some of the Caribbean's most beautiful destinations onboard Celebrity Beyond, one of our newest ships. This week-long cruise departs from Fort Lauderdale and includes two leisurely days at sea as well as five points of call.

Spend a day in Nassau lounging on one of the island's beautiful beaches. Snorkeling and scuba diving aficionados may visit one of the island's coral reefs to explore an underwater world teeming with colorful animals. Go shopping at the famed Nassau Straw Market, where you'll discover a wide range of local and handcrafted things that would make ideal Christmas presents.

Spend the day in Costa Maya at one of the beach clubs, where you may relax on the sand or participate in water activities like kayaking and snorkeling. Visit the ancient Mayan remains at Chacchoben, which include pyramids, temples, and expansive gardens. Alternatively, take the kids to the Lost Mayan Kingdom, a local water park with slides, zip lines, and river tubing, for a great day.

Spend Thanksgiving Day in Cozumel, where you can snorkel among vivid coral reefs, shop in San Miguel, or visit the ruins of Tulum, another Mayan citadel, where you may marvel at ancient constructions set against the background of the sea.

Search for starfish and swim with stingrays, jet-ski or parasail, or dive or snorkel throughout your day in Grand Cayman. You may also take a tour of the Cayman Turtle Center or just relax on the beach with a book. You'll spend one more day at sea before returning to Fort Lauderdale, allowing you to make use of the ship's exquisite facilities.

Before settling down with your family for another scrumptious meal in one of Beyond's world-class restaurants, enjoy a peaceful spa visit or an exciting shopping expedition, recline on the sundeck, or participate in water sports in the pool.

Chapter-24

9 Places to Visit on New Year's Eve in 2022

What better way to ring in 2022 than with an unforgettable vacation to a breathtaking location? There's a great New Year's trip for every style of traveler, from low-key parties to more daring adventures. This is an excellent time to take a bucket-list vacation, go outside of your comfort zone, see that vista you've always imagined in person, or experience your favorite meal prepared in its homeland. There are numerous possibilities for honoring a new year, whether you're looking for a spot to rest after the holidays, a more bustling city getaway to celebrate or wide-open landscapes with a side of spectacular scenery. Here are nine destinations to visit for New Year's Eve in 2022 that will get your year off to a great start.

This article includes the following sections:

St. Kitts and Nevis

After the Christmas rush, a calm beach break is just what you need. With pristine beaches, turquoise waters, and lots of warm sunlight, the Caribbean island of St. Kitts is ready to give a calm escape to decompress. One of the nicest things to do in St. Kitts is to go to Cockleshell Beach, which is situated on the island's southern shore and offers excellent views of Nevis, St. Kitts' sister island. Soft sand gives a postcard-perfect background for reading, walking, or enjoying a leisurely snooze in the sun, while calm waves call for a dip.

For snacks and drinks, there are several cafés along the beach. As little waves wash the coast, dine on delicious seafood at one of these eateries, providing the perfect setting for a laid-back New Year's party in paradise. When you've gotten your fill of beach relaxation, the pristine waters, which are home to offshore shipwrecks and an abundance of marine life, welcome snorkeling and diving aficionados. Alternatively, stretch your legs on the trekking track that climbs to Mount Liamuiga, St. Kitts' highest peak. This hike will reward you with breath-taking panoramic vistas. Do you want to spend some time at the spa? This is an ideal location for health-conscious vacationers.

Ring in the New Year with all of your worries from the previous year dissipated. Cheers to 2022 with some local rum after a full island day. This is one of the most popular New Year's Eve destinations.

Singapore

Singapore is a dynamic alternative for a fast-paced city trip with practically everything at your fingertips for ringing in the New Year in style. Enjoy the city's gastronomy, wildlife, and seashore attractions while admiring the city's creative architecture. The cuisine scene is out of this world, influenced by Chinese, Malay, and Indian civilizations. Street food fans will be in culinary paradise, with plenty of genuine delights to choose from. Try Hainanese chicken rice, char kway teow, and kaya toast, which are all local favorites.

If you only have three days in Singapore during the holidays, make the most of it by visiting the world-famous botanical gardens, which are a UNESCO World Heritage Site. The enormous diversity of flora and wildlife will astound you, especially the large orchid garden, which boasts the world's largest collection of orchids. The well-known Singapore Flyer, a Ferris wheel affording an incredible vision of one of the greatest skylines in the world, offers a bird's-eye view of the city. The lights will amaze you on your voyage into the skies at night.

Dominican Republic, Puerto Plata

Consider the coastal town of Puerto Plata on the Dominican Republic's northern coast whether lazing on the beach or starting on an exciting adventure is your idea of the ideal end of the year. Relaxed beaches and lush forests combine to provide an ideal balance of relaxation and exhilaration.

You may choose from a variety of beaches, including Playa Sosa, which has a view of Mount Isabel de Torres, and Playa Dorada, which is one of the most well-known. If you're looking for a thrill, go to Cabarete Beach, one of the top kitesurfing beaches in the Dominican Republic. Discover the Damajagua Waterfalls, one of the island's most popular and beautiful natural attractions. The limestone cliffs, tunnels, and cascade of 27 waterfalls are awe-inspiring. Cool yourself in natural ponds that seem to be secluded and tucked away in another universe.

This climb will make you feel like a genuine adventurer, offering both adrenaline and beauty, making it one of the greatest things to do in Puerto Plata.

The Galapagos Islands are a group of islands off the coast of Ecuador

For wildlife lovers, the famed Galapagos Islands off the coast of Ecuador are the perfect bucket-list vacation. This secluded group of islands is a great place to ring in the New Year, with unlimited animal watching chances in a surreal atmosphere. Sea lions, giant tortoises, playful penguins, and indigenous marine species may all be found on the Galapagos Islands, which are protected.

Blue-footed boobies, sea turtles, and whale sharks will usher in the New Year. Snorkelers will love Isla Lobos and San Christobal, while hikers will love going crater hiking in Sierra Negra. You'll want to have your camera handy at all times to record the stunning surroundings and fascinating animal interactions you'll have here.

Florida's Key West

Key West is the perfect place to celebrate the New Year with a mix of excitement and sun. If you want to ring in the year 2022 like Ernest Hemingway, go to Florida's southernmost point. Swim, snorkel, and wander along Duval Street for a wide variety of cuisine and drink.

Visit Ernest Hemingway's home, a Spanish Colonial mansion that is now a museum. Meet and greet the property's famed six-toed cats. Explore the neighboring historic Fort Jefferson at Dry Tortugas National Park, and don't forget to take a picture at the concrete buoy that marks the continental United States' southernmost point. A sunset cruise is a popular way to see Key West and see some of the most beautiful sunsets in the country. In Key West, Florida, toast the New Year with a piece of the key lime pie.

Patagonia

The area of Patagonia in South America is one of the greatest locations to travel to for New Year's Eve if you like the outdoors and breathtaking vistas.

The Andes mountain range is the main attraction, with glacial-fed lakes, fjords, deserts, and grasslands thrown in for good measure, contributing to the natural attractiveness. Tierra del Fuego National Park, located just outside of Ushuaia, offers a unique environment to explore. Local fauna like red foxes and guanacos are surrounded by moss-covered forests, rivers, and glacial lakes. Immerse yourself in nature by trekking one of the park's routes to awe-inspiring locations like the Black Lagoon or the Lapataia Bay vantage point.

Take the train to "the end of the earth" for a completely comfortable approach to take in the sights. The Southern Fuegian Railway's steam train excursion is an excellent chance to take in the natural beauty of Patagonia's southernmost section. While admiring the gorgeous South American waterfalls, mountains, and animals, you'll learn about the region's history. One of the most unique ways to celebrate the New Year is to go to the furthest reaches of the globe.

The Virgin Islands, United States of America

A sumptuous Caribbean trip will allow you to ring in the New Year on the beach. The U.S. Virgin Islands are made up of the lovely islands of St. Thomas, St. John, and St. Croix, which are bursting with stunning beaches, turquoise waters, and entertaining activities to keep everyone in your party amused.

Snorkeling with sea turtles, island hopping, and hiking in the national park are all options. Magen's Bay on St. Thomas, Trunk Bay Beach on St. John, and Christiansted Beach on St. Croix are among the nicest beaches in the Caribbean. Admire the views from the islands, savor Caribbean cuisine, toast the new year with native island rum, and relax in the laid-back atmosphere.

Bangkok is the capital of Thailand

Thailand is an excellent option for a unique New Year's party. Authentic cultural experiences, incredible culinary delights, and dynamic city life are just a few of the exciting things to look forward to in Bangkok, one of the greatest cities to visit on New Year's Eve.

Visit Wat Arun, Wat Phra Kaew, and the Temple of Dawn in Bangkok for at least two days to marvel at the exquisite Khmer architecture and attention to ornamental details. You'll visit Thai marketplaces, palaces, and museums as you cruise along the Chao Phraya River. Visiting Bangkok's floating market is a must-do. This well-known artisan and products experience is a multi-sensory delight. Watch as tiny boats laden with fruit, home-cooked meals, and handcrafted items sail the rivers, selling their products.

New Zealand is a country in the Pacific Ocean

New Zealand has some of the most beautiful scenery and experiences in the world, making it one of the most fantastic destinations to visit for New Year's. Put on your hiking boots and take an exciting hike on one of the country's excellent walking trails to ring in the New Year.

Sip your way through world-class vineyards in New Zealand, such as the Marlborough wine area, which produces some of the greatest sauvignon blanc, pinot noir, and chardonnay in the world. Sail through the beautiful Fiordland area, where the famed Milford Sound greets you with jaw-dropping scenery and more waterfalls than you can count.

On a luxury cruise holiday, see some of the world's top spots to celebrate New Year's Eve. A New Year's cruise is a terrific way to make the most of your 2022 celebration, whether you're looking for a refreshing beach getaway, starting off the New Year with some fresh air and fitness, gourmet delights, or an immersive cultural city experience. On our website, you may look at cruise itineraries and book your holiday cruise trip right now.

Chapter-25

In 2022, there are 8 incredible places to spend Christmas on the beach

If you like traveling, you're undoubtedly looking forward to the next opportunity to visit the beach. You could also yearn for the chance to go out of town for a few days around the holidays to relax with family and reflect on the year. It's never too early to start thinking about a Christmas beach getaway. It's the ideal time of year to go away from the cold for a few days in the sun in a tropical location.

Here are some of the greatest beach destinations for Christmas in 2022. Also, don't assume you have to skip out on a Christmas tree or a family supper. You may still party all day, but there will be a little more sun and sand than normal. After all, it's Christmas at the beach.

Nassau is the capital of the Bahamas
Set your eyes on Nassau, Bahamas, for a fast trip from just about anyplace on the east coast. Nassau is one of the most accessible destinations from the United States, yet it doesn't seem like anything you'd find in the United States. It's bright, warm, and inviting, and the cuisine is delicious, so it's a great spot to spend Christmas on the beach if you want to skip the mashed potatoes in favor of ceviche.

Spend the day at the Atlantis Resort, which has some of Nassau's greatest beaches and packs an unbelievable amount of action into one massive place, for a really unique Christmas. Walkthrough a shark tank (or ride a waterslide through one), visit the Aquaventure Water Park, swim with dolphins, or rent a private cabana for two by the pool or beach. Around the holidays, there are lots of events for both families and adults.

Book a journey to Balmoral Island, just off the coast, for a unique Christmas Day celebration. Beach loungers, snorkel gear rentals, a restaurant and bar, and chances to swim with stingrays and dolphins are all available at the exclusive beach resort. The island is just a short boat journey away, and beach floats and tubes are available so you may spend your Christmas relaxing in the sun.

Aside from beach activities, spend the day visiting the Bahama Barrels Winery, which is set on the grounds of a historic church from the 1930s. Because it's difficult to produce grapes in the Bahamas, the winery imports grapes from all around the globe to create exceptional mixes and varietals on-site. A tour, a hands-on winemaking session, and even the opportunity to create your own bespoke blend are all included in most visits—now that's a fantastic Christmas gift.

Curacao
Scuba divers and snorkelers looking for a beach vacation this Christmas should visit Curacao, where the on-land activities are fantastic, but the underwater world is much better. Spend Christmas Day at Blue Bay Beach, where you'll discover beachfront massages, beach bars, restaurants, and sand loungers with thatched sunshades, as well as water activities like snorkeling and kayaking. One of the nicest things to do in Curaçao is to take a sunset catamaran trip to toast a wonderful day with loved ones as the sunsets.

You might also go to Mambo Beach, a well-developed and popular beach not far from Willemstad, to discover your beach pleasure. Mambo Beach is a terrific choice if you want to spend some time on the beach with your toes in the sand while also doing some shopping and eating. The beach offers fantastic snorkeling and scuba diving opportunities, as well as a cove sheltered by rocks if you're traveling with children or want a calmer environment.

On the promenade just off the beach, there are lots of restaurants, stores, and boutiques, so if you need a break from the heat, you can go into a small artisan shop and pick out the ideal Christmas gift—for friends or for yourself.

Cozumel

Cozumel is a must-see destination any time of year, with its magnificent beaches, scuba diving and snorkeling options, fantastic outdoor experiences, and historical history. But spending Christmas on the beach here, sipping fresh coconut juice while watching dolphins swim just offshore, seems exceptionally exotic and beautiful.

If your vacation objective is to spend as much time as possible on the beach, Playa Mia may be the place for you. There's more just off the sand than a wide-open beach, sun chairs and loungers, kayaks, snorkel gear, and even an inflatable over-the-water obstacle course for adults. Several pools, a lazy river, a hydro-massage hot tub, and, of course, a swim-up cocktail bar are among the amenities. Because the weather in Cozumel is generally always warm and bright, you may want to try a tequila sunrise instead of your traditional Christmas hot toddy.

Cozumel remains a favorite choice for those seeking a more adventurous vacation. San Gervasio, devoted to the birth and fertility goddess Ix Chel, and Chichen Itza, a vast Mayan metropolis finally taken over by the Spanish in the mid-1500s, are two Mayan sites near Cozumel. For a resort so near to the United States, Cozumel provides the opportunity to experience a Christmas unlike any other.

Jamaica

Is there a more laid-back island location or one with a happy population than Jamaica? Is there anything more opulent than being able to declare, "This Christmas, we'll be spending it on the beach in Montego Bay?"

Relax in the warm sun of Montego Bay for the day, particularly if the entire goal of your well-deserved vacation is to spend Christmas at the beach. Relax on the sand at Doctor's Cave Beach, browse the stores and boutiques right off the beach, or throw a frisbee into the sea before stopping for a pia colada. You might alternatively spend the day lounging in a private cabana at the Bamboo Beach Club. Send a photo of your feet on the sand to your friends and family back home.

Consider going to Blue Water Beach if you want to spend your Christmas at the beach in a more low-key manner. It's a little farther out of Montego Bay, and it's not as busy, but it's just as lovely. More than simply the beach, the area surrounding the beach is famed for its local jerk chicken businesses and reggae musicians at local pubs, so it's definitely worth a visit.

Waterfalls abound in Jamaica, and they play an important part in the island's enjoyment. You may visit Dunn's River Falls, which is officially one waterfall but seems to be a big multi-stepped cascade due to enormous stones and trees sprouting up around the flowing water. This location is one of the top trekking spots in the Caribbean. You may also take a tour inside the Green Grotto Caves, a system built over thousands of years by water flow. Deep inside the cave, there is even an underground lake.

St. Kitts and Nevis
St. Kitts is the place to go for an English-inspired Christmas (with a dash of island flair thrown in for good measure). St. Kitts was home to the first British and French colonies in the Caribbean in the mid-1600s, and the English Queen is still the symbolic head of state, even though Saint Kitts and Nevis is a sovereign state. As a result, it preserves much of its English culture, including streets that resemble those in London. It is, nonetheless, authentically Caribbean, home to Creole cuisine, private beaches, and interior jungle.

Spend Christmas on Cockleshell Bay Beach, a laid-back stretch of sand peppered with low-key island beach bars. Because there are no formalities here, you'll most likely be spending Christmas alongside friendly locals who are also enjoying a beach day on one of the Caribbean's greatest white-sand beaches.

You may alternatively spend Christmas morning on the beach and spend the afternoon riding the St. Kitts Scenic Railway. It's a two-decker open-air train that takes you through the island's crops, lush woodland, and panoramic shoreline. If trains aren't your thing, try a catamaran or a trek up Mount Liamuiga, one of the Caribbean's highest peaks. You can't go wrong with what you do each day when you're spending the week or so around Christmas at the beach.

St. Croix is a small island in the Caribbean
Because St. Croix is the biggest of the United States Virgin Islands, it boasts more beaches than the others. On Christmas Day, travel to Buck Island for a great combination of action and leisure. Beautiful beaches with silky white sand and azure blue sea may be found on the little island.

What's more, the reef here has been declared as a national monument, and you may go on an underwater snorkel "tour" of the ocean scenery. As you swim through the reefs, you can expect to encounter anything from small shrimp to three-foot-long sea turtles, making it the greatest Virgin Island to visit for snorkelers and divers.

You may also spend Christmas at Rainbow Beach, a laid-back beach not far from Frederiksted. The ocean is tranquil, and there are lots of spots to lay down a beach towel and umbrella for a few hours on the gently sloping sand. You may swim and float in the water, although there are a few portions of underwater rocks where little marine life can be seen on occasion.

You'll like it if you wish to spend the whole day relaxing on the beach. You can also hire kayaks, paddleboards, or even jet skis to explore the coast if you want a bit more excitement.

Cayman Islands

Some of the best beaches in the world may be found in Grand Cayman. Seven Mile Beach, which is really a continuous succession of beaches, coves, and magnificent views, is one of those beaches. It's a fantastic length of sand to spend the holiday season on since you can spend the whole day there. Relax for a few hours on a beach lounger, go snorkeling, or stop by a local beach bar for an afternoon beverage. After that, take a walk down the beach and look for neighboring coves and tidepools. You could even spot a marine turtle or two in the shallow water if you're fortunate.

It may not seem attractive to go to Hell on Christmas Day, but it is when you're in Grand Cayman. The "Hell" rock formation is a scenic area of the island where black limestone rocks spread, producing a panorama reminiscent of Dante's "Inferno."

You may also spend Christmas morning on Grand Cayman slightly west of the beach, which puts you right in the midst of the water. Take a short boat journey to Stingray City, a beach just off the coast where stingrays and nurse sharks often gather. They're accustomed to humans, and the water is shallow enough that you can jump off the boat with snorkel gear and swim only a few feet above them. These relaxed creatures are more interested in the little bits of food floating close than in you.

St. Thomas is the patron saint of sailors

Another fantastic choice for a seaside Christmas is St. Thomas. Is there a more suitable place to spend Christmas than a beach named "Christmas Cove?" The little bay is the picture-perfect spot for a day of relaxation, whether you're reading a book on the beach, swimming in the turquoise-blue water, or snorkeling among rock formations searching for turtles. You may still eat an island-inspired Christmas meal at one of the neighboring beach restaurants.

As lovely as Christmas Cove seems for a vacation, Sapphire Beach also looks appealing. Sapphire Beach is a wide-open beach surrounded by the same crystal blue sea as Christmas Cove, although it is a bit farther away from the downtown districts. Book a beach club or tour that includes amenities such as loungers, snorkeling equipment, and a memorable fresh fruit cocktail.

A deluxe Christmas cruise will take you to the beach next winter. You'll be transported from one beautiful beach spot to the next while enjoying world-class cuisine, unparalleled service, and festive holiday decorations on board.

Chapter-26

11 Spectacular Places to Visit on Your Birthday

Birthdays are a time to rejoice, and we are fortunate in that we have one every year. Traveling for a birthday can be a terrific way to celebrate, especially if it's the start of a new decade—turning 40 or 50 is surely cause for celebration! It's possible to get away on your birthday for more than just a good time. It's an opportunity to reflect on the previous year, plan for the coming year, and take a few days to focus on yourself.

It's never too early to start planning birthday trips, even if your birthday is months away. Here are some romantic, thrilling, and stunning birthday destinations from around the world.

Barcelona, Spain

When people are asked which city they enjoy the best, Barcelona is frequently mentioned. Beaches, history, incredible food, romance, beautiful architecture, art, and more abound in this Catalan city. This is not a city where you have to put in a lot of effort to keep your days busy. Barcelona is one of the greatest destinations to visit for your birthday if you want to do a lot of different things on one trip. Start your day with a sightseeing tour of the city's most iconic structures, such as Casa Battló, Park Güell, and La Sagrada Familia, designed by Antoni Gaud.

Alternatively, you may spend the morning lounging on the beach or taking a leisurely stroll through the old Barri Gotic (Gothic Quarter.) Take a tapas-and-wine-pairing tour or stop by one of the many little cafés along Las Ramblas for lunch. The possibilities are unlimited, so if Barcelona is at the top of your list of birthday trip destinations, here's how to spend three days in the city.

Venice, Italy

In Venice, romance is constantly present; after all, what could be more romantic than a sunset gondola ride down the city's famous canals? Consider planning a romantic holiday for two to the Italian city if your dream birthday revolves around a romantic retreat with your spouse or lover.

Of course, if you enjoy history or art, you'll be lured to this lovely city. Visit Doge's Palace, a 14th-century palace that once belonged to the Venitian Republic's leader. Then, before traveling to St. Mark's Square, take a walk through Venice's hidden and twisting lanes, stopping to see centuries-old glass-blowing studios. The city appears to have been created specifically for couples in love. Of all, a candlelit cobblestone street in the heart of Italy is hard to beat for a romantic dining setting.

Bermuda

Bermuda is truly a one-of-a-kind destination for east coasters searching for a quick tropical escape. It feels more luxurious than other resorts because of the mix of British influence and tropical environs. Bermuda is one of the finest birthday trips for another reason: its trademark pink sand. While amazing shopping and eating opportunities are a given, Bermuda is also one of the best birthday trips for another reason: it is signature pink sand.

Some of the top Bermuda beaches are known not just for their beauty—bright blue ocean and rocky coves ensure that nearly all of the island's beaches are breathtaking—but also for their pink sand, which you won't find in many other places. Horseshoe Bay, one of Bermuda's most famous beaches, entices visitors with its moderate waves and picture-perfect views.

You may spend your birthday in Bermuda resting on the beach with a rum swizzle in hand, then spend the next day exploring an underground crystal grotto or taking a catamaran tour of the shoreline.

Vancouver, British Columbia, Canada

If you live in California or the Pacific Northwest and are seeking amazing birthday travel ideas, consider heading north to breathtakingly beautiful Vancouver. The beach on one side and the mountains on the other, with a tropical rainforest not far away, define the seaside metropolis. It's the perfect combination of urban luxury and outdoor adventure for anyone who enjoys hiking during the day and dining on a gourmet tasting menu at night.

One of British Columbia's most unforgettable experiences is crossing the Capilano Suspension Bridge, which is a must-see for anyone visiting the city. The lengthy suspension bridge, which stretches more than 100 feet above the rainforest floor, provides a bird's-eye perspective of the lush surroundings. It's great for people of all ages and abilities, and it's a great way to connect with nature in Vancouver without having to go on a long hike.

The Sea-to-Sky Gondola, which soars more than 2,000 feet into the air in the mountains of nearby Squamish, is another great way to see Vancouver's wild side. If you have time, go to neighboring Shannon Falls, where a short walking route leads to one of Western Canada's most impressive (and screaming) waterfalls.

Key West, Florida

If you're traveling with a group of friends, Key West in Florida is one of the greatest spots to celebrate your birthday. Low-key pubs are just stepped away from expensive spas and cafes in the Keys, so you can have a good time and appreciate the finer things in life. Though the vibrant seaport district near Duval Street is bustling with activity, it is a National Historic Landmark that was formerly frequented by prominent Key West residents such as Ernest Hemmingway.

Because Key West is one of the most tropical places in the United States, celebrate your birthday by getting out on the sea. Snorkeling and swimming with dolphins are two of the top activities to do in Key West with kids if you're visiting with family. There are dozens of tours and boat rentals to choose from, including catamarans sails to see dolphins in the wild and snorkeling tours to visit Key West's greatest coral reefs.

Bonaire

If you enjoy snorkeling or scuba diving, a trip to Bonaire, an island known for having some of the best diving in the world, is a must. On the island, there are more than 50 places where you may scuba dive or snorkel just off the shore. Grab your gear and head out to see some of the Caribbean's most colorful wildlife up close. What better location to celebrate your birthday than a coral reef?

There's much to do when you're not in the water. Kayaking through a mangrove river, learning to windsurf, and witnessing flamingos in the wild are just a few of the top things to do in Bonaire. Because Bonaire is a small island, you'll be able to spend your birthday riding an ATV, sunbathing on the beach, or sailing on a catamaran all within a few minutes of the capital, Kralendijk.

Mexico's Cozumel

Consider going to Cozumel to celebrate your birthday if you just have a few days. The ever-popular coastal city in Mexico is inexpensive, friendly, and full of opportunities to learn about the country's rich history and culture.

History aficionados may wish to spend their birthdays exploring Chichen Itza, the Mayan Empire's former capital, with its pyramids, temples, and tombs. Sign up for a couple's or small-group cooking class to get a taste of Mexico's current culture.

Snorkeling and catamaran cruises are always available if you wish to spend your birthday in Cozumel's warm waters. If you want to try something new for your birthday, you may take a dive class or go on an underwater expedition while wearing an astronaut-style helmet that provides air from the surface as you walk over the ocean bottom.

Quebec City, Canada

Consider visiting Old Quebec, on the banks of Canada's St. Lawrence River, for the charm of a European city. Don't be shocked if you're greeted with bonjour instead of hello, and menus are available in both French and English, as Quebec is known for being more French than the rest of Canada.

Old Quebec is beautiful, with white lights hanging from the windows, flower boxes hanging from the windows, and outside seating in front of every cafe. You may take a funicular down to walk the cobblestone alleyways of the ancient city, or you can enjoy a romantic horse-drawn trolley trip through the city. On your birthday, a food tour is a terrific chance to try something new, especially because Quebec City is recognized for its unique and modern blend of French and Canadian cuisines. If you've never had poutine, you should.

Curaçao

Curaçao is a little more urbanized version of Bonaire, and the two islands are almost neighbors. Curaçao, like Bonaire, has beautiful beaches and exciting watersports, but it also has a more developed downtown area in Willemstad, the capital city. Taking Caribbean food cooking classes (maybe to organize a delayed birthday party when you come home?), seeing an ostrich farm, or touring the 300,000-year-old Hato Caves are just a few of the top things to do in Curaçao.

Curaçao isn't quite as well-known as other islands, so it's one of the finest places to celebrate your birthday if you want to do something a little different and enjoy a great combination of beach relaxation and unique experiences.

Chapter-27

Everything You Need to Know About Purchasing Souvenirs in Port

There's a lot to love about a cruise vacation: the delectable food, the ability to relax and sunbathe in the sun, the exotic destinations on the itinerary, and the option to do some souvenir shopping in each port.

While you can buy t-shirts, refrigerator magnets, and baseball caps anywhere, one of the best things about buying souvenirs on a cruise is that you can find unique goods and presents in each port destination that will remind you of all the lovely places you visited.

Follow these recommendations for finding the best souvenirs while in port, as well as some guidance on customs and duty-free shopping.

Begin your investigation as soon as possible

Do some study on each of the countries and ports of call on your cruise itinerary before sailing. Find out about their signature products and see if there are any local foods or items that might make good gifts for family and friends back home. In Barbados, for example, you'll want to keep an eye out for beautiful ceramics. Don't forget to bring back a bottle of local tequila during your trip to Mexico.

Throughout the year, many cities and small communities host a variety of festivals and art fairs. To find unique souvenirs during your vacation, find out if your visit coincides with any local events.

Another simple approach to learning more about a country's culture is to go to its tourism board and chamber of commerce websites, which frequently include excellent information about unique local goods and shopping suggestions.

Make sure you understand what you're authorized to carry back to your home country. It's a good idea to check out ahead of time what you're allowed to bring back home and on the cruise ship once you've decided what you want to buy. Visit the US Customs & Border Patrol website for further information on what things are permitted and prohibited entry into the United States.

Seek advice

Once you're on board, the pleasant crew members on Celebrity are delighted to give you shopping advice and tell you about their favorite stores and shopping districts in each port. Similarly, ask locals you meet in different port places (for example, restaurant servers, taxi drivers, or shore excursion operators) if they know of any smaller stores that locals enjoy. During your voyage, you'll be given a port shopping tutorial as well as a map of stores.

You're in luck if you've booked one of Celebrity's Alaska or Caribbean cruises. Local retail districts have many establishments on the same block, making purchasing Alaska souvenirs in port particularly simple.

Look for duty-free shops

Duty-free shops can be found in several of our Caribbean and Bermuda cruise destinations. The local value-added tax (equivalent to a sales tax) is not included in the prices in these stores, which can be up to 33 percent of the item's price.

Taxes are already included in the pricing in many countries. Because alcohol, jewelry, and other luxury items are normally subject to a high tax, you may expect to get a fantastic deal at a duty-free shop. However, even in a duty-free shop, children's items are not duty-free.

Don't forget to declare your purchases

You must still declare all products purchased during your cruise trip when you return to the United States. If you go above the price limit (for further information, go to the US Borders and Customs website), you'll have to pay taxes on the extra items. Keep in mind that the amount of alcohol and cigarette items you can carry into the nation is likewise limited.

Consider food mementos

Don't forget about grocery stores, gourmet shops, and farmer's markets when looking for keepsakes. They're all great places to learn about the local culture and gastronomy while also picking up a unique souvenir to take home.

In major, foreign cities, port shopping for distinctive delicacies and gourmet items is very enjoyable. If you're taking a European cruise that docks in a large city, you'll find foods from all around the continent at the most well-stocked grocery stores. These will make a huge difference in your home kitchen when cooking meals, and they'll also make great gifts for friends and family.

Begin a collection

If you travel regularly, consider amassing a collection of a specific type of memento that can be found in various forms in each port you visit. Souvenir stores all across the world sell items like playing cards, ornaments, wind chimes, and straw hats.

Bring the appropriate currency

Merchants will accept U.S. dollars at various Caribbean, Asian, and Middle Eastern cruise ports, as well as in Mexico, but any change will be refunded in the local currency.

If you're traveling around Europe, you'll find that most shops in port cities don't accept dollars, so you'll need to find a convenient and cost-effective way to exchange money before you leave. Credit cards are accepted in some higher-end retailers, such as museum stores, art galleries, and designer boutiques. However, some credit card issuers charge a fee for foreign transactions, so keep that in mind while calculating and comparing prices.

Mother's Day Travel Gifts for Mom: 18 Ideas

If your mother was the one who initially inspired you to travel, thank her with one of these thoughtful Mother's Day travel presents. We've compiled a list of 18 of our favorite travel-themed accessories, gadgets, and other random goodies that will make Mom's travels easier, better, and more beautiful than ever.

This year's Mother's Day falls on Sunday, May 9, and there's no doubt that moms deserve a well-deserved gift following a particularly trying year. This wish list includes everything from utilitarian to inspirational items, as well as budget-friendly and splurge-worthy items. (As an added bonus, these thoughtful gifts for globetrotting moms are also appropriate for birthdays and holidays!) You'll not only warm Mom's heart with your thoughtfulness, but you'll also kindle her wanderlust if you give her one of these Mother's Day travel presents.

Basket & Cookbook

We all know that foodies may sometimes organize their entire holidays around a certain region's culinary scene. Consider replicating a taste of your mom's favorite trip locations right at home if her palate has to lead her to her next travel destination.

You may bring Mom's favorite culinary experiences back to her right on her own soil, whether she likes the cuisines of Italy, Thailand, or Turkey. Invest in an international cookbook as well as a basket of complementary products, such as sauces, spices, and other regional delicacies. A basket styled after Italy, for example, would include jars of high-quality sauces, organic pasta, and balsamic vinegar.

Alternatively, give her a gift certificate to a local ethnic restaurant where she can dine on regional delicacies that will transport her back to her favorite vacation places.

Passport Cover with Personalization

When it comes to travel, pulling out your passport signifies that you're about to go on an adventure to a faraway nation (or are returning home from a recent journey). Make Mom's special day even more special by giving her a chic, personalized passport holder.

They come in a variety of forms and sizes but go for one of the elegant leather varieties. For further personalization, you may have your mother's initials monogrammed directly on the front.

Upgrade to a larger, more stylish travel wallet so Mom can safely store her passport, as well as IDs, cards, and travel documents. This practical present combines polish with the utmost in the organization, allowing Mom to keep all of her important documents in one location.

Delivery to the Wine Country

Bring wine country to the oenophile mama in your life if she can't get to wine country. Many of the world's most prestigious vineyards provide direct shipment, and there are a plethora of customized wine subscription services that make excellent Mother's Day trip gifts. She'll be taken to the vines of her favorite wine area vineyards if she stocks up on her preferred varietals.

It doesn't matter if she's been missing Napa, Mendoza, Bordeaux, or somewhere else. After all, with all of her hard work, we know Mom might benefit from a bottle of wine (or two).

The hat that folds up for travel

A decent, wide-brimmed hat that offers protection from the sun's rays is important if Mom is going someplace sunny, be it the beach, a national park, or even a city sightseeing excursion. However, some of the most attractive hats are difficult to pack, so do your mother a favor and select one that is designed for travel.

Several packable travel hats are available on the market that can be simply rolled up or folded into a bag or purse. Choose one that is elegant and adaptable enough to be worn with a sundress or a swimsuit. Hopefully, your mother would compliment you on your thoughtful gift.

Books on Travel Photography

By glancing through a good art or photo book, armchair travelers can easily become immersed in the locales they fantasize about. Travel photographers have a knack for capturing the essence of a place by depicting snippets of life through street scenes, portraiture, cultural events, and natural surroundings.

Pick up a couple of art books about a favorite vacation spot for Mom, and let her relive or imagine a place that makes her heart sing. Beautiful photo books can portray Greek beaches, Alaskan wilderness, New York City's concrete jungle, and just about anything else you can imagine.

Cooking Class on the Internet

Consider giving Mom a virtual cooking class if she enjoys being in the kitchen. She can easily join a local chef-led class on the opposite side of the planet thanks to the technical adaptability of today's video-centric culture.

Mom will have no trouble finding a class that suits her tastes, whether it's Peruvian ceviche, Spanish tapas, or Argentinian empanadas. She'll not only get to take part in an immersive cooking session where she'll meet great local chefs and like-minded foodies, but she'll also walk away with some new culinary skills.

Case for Traveling with Jewelry

A small travel jewelry bag, whether it's a roll-up design or a hard mini-container, is vital for the parent who loves her baubles. Earring, ring, necklace and bracelet sections are devoted and zippered in the better ones, ensuring that Mom's favorite accessories are safely stowed away, tangle-free, and quick to turn up.

If you really want to impress her, team up with a local jewelry designer in a region she adores and have a piece put away in her case. Many jewelry designers now have an online store and can easily ship internationally. Encourage Mom to travel with the case half-full so she can load up on jewelry findings to bring home as souvenirs from her next trip.

Bag for the Weekend

Your travel-loving mother's luggage is probably in order, but there's always room for a new, trendy weekender bag. Whether she's looking for a nice carry-on for her next flight or a bag that's just ideal for a quick weekend excursion, these multipurpose carryalls come in all shapes and sizes.

Choose one with a striking design that she will adore, and it will also serve as a fashion statement. Whatever you choose, make sure it's light and spacious enough to hold all of her essentials, and you'll have a winning Mother's Day travel present that will delight her.

Travel Aromatherapy Kit

Travel is fantastic in many ways, but that doesn't mean it isn't stressful or exhausting. Whether you're suffering from jet lag, lack of energy, or need some assistance falling asleep, there's an essential oil combination for you. Travel-size roller balls are ideal since they can be tucked into Mom's carry-on for a convenient pick-me-up for body, mind, and spirit.

Organizers for Luggage

If your mother is a neat freak, she'll appreciate items that will make her travels go more smoothly. Packing cubes are revolutionary if she hasn't already discovered them. These space-saving cubes will not only free up more suitcase room but will also make it easier for her to find what she's looking for. It's also a good idea to invest in a useful digital travel kit organizer so Mom can neatly store all of her favorite gadgets.

Scarf for Traveling

The most flexible item in Mom's suitcase might be a fashionable, lightweight travel scarf. Travel scarves are versatile, whether she's wearing it as an extra layer on a chilly day, turning it into a pillow-in-a-pinch for a long journey, or utilizing it as a beautiful wrap to dress up an outfit for a night out. Choose a scarf, sarong, or blanket in a color that your mother adores, and make it out of popular fabrics like cashmere, wool, or silk, and your mother will have all she needs for her next vacation.

An Online Course to Improve Travel Skills

If your mother is the sort to never stop learning, there's a good chance you'll be able to locate an online course that she'll enjoy. Whether she's always wanted to learn a new language, improve her photography skills, or develop a new interest in Japanese gardening, match her with the ideal class to make her next major trip even more memorable.

Journal of Travel

Even in an age of limitless technology and devices, there's no alternative for capturing a moment with pen and paper. Mom can jot down her travel thoughts, sketch a picture of a favorite area, or plan out her travel itinerary for the day ahead in a sleek, tuck-away travel journal. Journals come in a variety of forms, with covers ranging from high art to old leather. She'll enjoy going back to this journal keepsake in the future to recall her first impressions from a beloved vacation.

Charger on the Go

While a portable charger may not appear to be a particularly interesting presentation on the surface, you'll be doing your mother a tremendous service by introducing her to the portable charger's life-saving capabilities. Find one that's slim and elegant, so Mom can toss it in her bag before heading off on her next journey. When the device charges her phone or camera when she's out and about and in need of a boost, she'll be screaming your praises.

Travel Poster or Print

Does Mom wax lyrical about her days spent in Italy?
Or when she learned to dance the tango in Argentina on her honeymoon?

Purchase a gorgeous travel print or poster that portrays a favorite place to help her easily relive those happy memories. You can find several art prints and travel posters online, and with a little web sleuthing, you can even connect with local artists for something more unique.

Eye Mask with Lavender

Travel normally entails a significant amount of travel time, and those minutes on trains and aircraft can provide a much-needed opportunity to sleep. A portable lavender eye mask can help Mom make the most of it by blocking out light, providing gentle compression acupressure, and providing aromatherapy. (Lavender is known for its calming properties and is claimed to aid with sleep and stress reduction.) Consider getting her a velvet version for the ultimate enjoyment.

Photo Albums in Hardcover

We sometimes lose sight of the old-school joy of having a real photo album to flick through on the spur of the moment in this digital age. Print Mom's best vacation photos and place them in a high-quality hardcover picture album. You'll be assisting her in preserving her priceless vacation memories, as well as inspiring her to create new ones in the future.

Donation to a charity

Consider foregoing a personal visit in favor of a Mother's Day travel present that will have an even greater impact.

Make a donation in your mother's name to a travel place close to her heart that needs assistance, whether it's a hurricane-ravaged region in the Caribbean or an orphanage in Asia. Not only will Mom be moved by your kindness, but your gift will also be a positive force in the world. That'll be tough to beat!

Mother's Day Cruises can be found here

While all of these gifts are wonderful, there is no better gift than a trip for a travel-obsessed mother. Give her the unforgettable experience of a cruise holiday with Cruises. Consider giving her the ideal Mother's Day travel present this year by looking through itineraries from all across the world.

For Father's Day, here are 14 great travel gifts for Dad

If your father is happiest when he's on the road, Father's Day is the ideal time to give him a travel-themed gift that will make him smile. After all, your dear old father has plenty of ties and coffee mugs at this point. Instead, keep your jet-setting father comfortable and engaged with these great Father's Day travel presents, which range from practical to sensational—and from budget-friendly to splurge-worthy.

While Father's Day is quickly approaching, these thoughtful gift ideas for Dad are also appropriate for birthdays and holidays. Here are 14 clever travel presents for Dad that are equal parts fun, cool, and functional, whether he travels for business or pleasure—or a little bit of both.

Vintage Poster of a Journey

If your father enjoys the golden age of travel, he'll appreciate the beautiful design and nostalgic appeal of vintage travel posters. Look for retro posters that accentuate the grandeur of metropolitan places like Paris and New York, or pick up a vintage poster that captures the attraction of tropical destinations like Mexico and Fiji. There are a plethora of possibilities available through online merchants. Choose one that depicts a place that holds a particular place in Dad's heart. You'll fly high in his eyes if you present the poster in a beautiful frame.

Backpack with Anti-Theft Device

A good backpack is a must-have for any busy dad. Improve your father's worry-free travel game with a high-quality anti-theft bag that boasts not just durability, functionality, comfort, and style, but also security features. Anti-theft backpacks contain anti-slash exteriors, wire-inlay straps, and sections that securely lock up to deter thieves. They're ideal for keeping travel essentials like phones, cameras, and travel documents close to reaching. A high-security pack is the next best thing until you can give dad an additional set of eyes for the back of his head.

Leather Toiletry Bag with Monogram

A toiletry bag is a must-have travel accessory, but that doesn't mean it has to be all about function. Upgrade Dad's travel kit with a high-quality leather toiletry bag that he can proudly carry on his many journeys and stuff full of all of his bathroom essentials. Offer some creative monogramming to this excellent travel present for dad to add a final touch that feels extra personal.

Grooming Products for Travel

When it comes to toiletry bags, they're only as excellent as the contents inside. Make sure Dad has all of his grooming requirements by giving him a selection of travel-size, airline-friendly, and suitcase-ready items that are far superior to a boring bar of hotel soap. Whether you buy a pre-assembled kit or put up a custom selection of his favorite items, make sure to include everything he needs to keep his skin, hair, teeth, and body looking and feeling great. Consider including travel beard kits with essentials like shaving cream and beard oil if Dad has a beard or mustache.

Bonus: Assisting Dad with TSA-approved toiletry needs ahead of time will guarantee that he is carry-on-ready for his next travel, saving him the time and money of having to check a bag. You're also saving him a trip to the local drugstore at his location, allowing him to savor every last second of his vacation time.

Luggage Locator

If you travel frequently enough, there's a good risk that one of your luggage will be temporarily misplaced by an airline. This has long been a prevalent travel problem with few solutions other than a lot of patience and a little luck. Today's technology, in the form of GPS (Global Position System)-enabled luggage trackers, has risen to the occasion. When Dad straps one of these smart luggage trackers to his bag, he won't have to rely on airline customer service.

Because it uses satellite technology to locate the bag's specific location, the small device helps protect against an unfortunate lost-luggage scenario. Your father will be able to track the bag with the touch of a button by just launching an app on his phone. (Keep in mind that some devices will require a separate subscription to use this feature.) What could be a nicer present than a little peace of mind?

Speaker with Bluetooth

With a tuck-away Bluetooth speaker that's excellent for travel, turn your dad into a DJ-on-the-go. Dad will be able to listen to his favorite music while relaxing in a hotel room, relaxing on the beach, or pitching a tent with the help of a portable speaker.

After all, life is that much better for music lovers when there is a perfect soundtrack to accompany it. Bluetooth speakers that are small enough to fit in the palm of your hand, weigh well under a pound, and have deceivingly fantastic sound are available. Consider speakers that are water- and sand-resistant if Dad enjoys being outside. When purchasing a portable speaker, don't scrimp on battery life. Make sure you get one that allows you to play for a long time on a single charge.

Cubes for packing

Packing cubes may not seem like an exciting Father's Day travel present, but for the uninitiated, this travel gear is revolutionary. Gifting a set of packing cubes to Dad will help him get his trip life in order, ensuring that his suitcase is as organized as they come. Shorts and slacks go in one cube, T-shirts in another, and he can sort from there. These cubes come in a variety of sizes to best suit his travel needs. Not only do the handy cubes help you stay organized, but they also help you get the most out of your luggage space.

Coffee Press for Travel

No coffee connoisseur should ever be without a good cup of their favorite caffeinated beverage. Fortunately, there are small coffee presses on the market that Dad can take with him on his next trip away from home, whether he's seeking the ideal cup of joe in an exotic hotel room or at the top of a mountain.

Look for models that can make American-style coffee, espresso, or cold brew (or all three), and make sure he has a travel-size container of his favorite coffee to go with it. Plus, certain coffee presses can also be used as drinking mugs.

Travel Pillow

Getting some rest while traveling can mean the difference between feeling great and feeling groggy when you arrive at your destination. Help Dad make the most of his next long aircraft, train, or bus voyage with a comfortable travel pillow. There are a variety of types to pick from, but for the best on-the-go dozing, go for one that provides adequate support and plenty of comforts while being compact and lightweight. Your father's neck and back will thank you later.

Organizer for Technology

Anyone who travels these days knows that every backpack has a plethora of electronic gizmos and gadgets, as well as the numerous wires and chargers that come with them. Give Dad a good tech organizer so he can tuck everything away neatly and safely. When he needs his phone charger, memory cards, USB flash drive, headphones, and other items, he'll be able to find them all neatly tucked away in this type of organizer. It has never been easier to travel.

Luggage Tags with Your Name

Luggage tags are an essential element of any trip. Make Dad a personalized, jazzed-up luggage tag that will elevate his suitcases to new heights. Dad won't have to scratch his head as look-alikes swirl around the airport carousel with a unique luggage tag affixed to his suitcase. There are countless styles to select from for these excellent travel gifts for dad but seek one that's durable as well as distinctive enough that he's likely to identify as his own.

For the ideal personalized touch, a gorgeous leather luggage tag with his monogrammed initials is a must.

In His Honor, a Charitable Donation

What do you gift for the man who has it all? The best answer is sometimes none at all. Instead, find a gift that speaks to dad's good nature and love of travel by supporting a cause in a place he enjoys visiting. Perhaps you'll donate to a disaster relief operation in the Caribbean or to a charity in Africa that helps rehabilitate wild animals. Whatever you choose, it will be a gift that you and your partner will cherish for a long time.

Charger on the Go

Nothing ruins a wonderful holiday day like running out of batteries for your camera or phone, yet no one wants to spend their vacation chained to an outlet. Make sure Dad doesn't end up in either of these situations by giving him a small and lightweight portable charger so he can get a burst of power whenever he needs it.

While all of these presents are likely to impress Dad on Father's Day, nothing beats an amazing trip for someone who likes to travel. Start arranging a Celebrity Cruises holiday today by browsing our itineraries throughout the world.

12 Gifts for the Cruiser in Your Life

Are you looking for the ideal cruise present for the globetrotter in your life? Holidays, anniversaries, and other special occasions may prompt your loved ones to take a cruise. Your best buddy might gather the ladies and throw a large birthday bash for you. Your digital nomad friends might want to celebrate PRIDE in style with a luxury vacation. There are a plethora of thoughtful gift ideas available for each occasion.

To get you started, here are a few cruise gift ideas.

Traveling Equipment

Those important people in your life who travel frequently are likely to want new accessories from time to time. Jetsetters, after all, put their luggage, adaptors, and travel gear to the ultimate test. Give a sleek leather passport holder or a minimalist, travel-sized bag intended to fit a phone, wallet, and keys. Invest them in new luggage and packing cubes for them to make packing and organizing a breeze. You might even include a few travel essentials in a larger gift basket.

Travel Accessories

No matter where they are going in the world, travel devices are always a must-have. Consider giving them a portable charger so they don't have to worry about running out of energy, a pair of Bluetooth headphones so they can listen to their favorite music, or a waterproof smartphone case to keep their phone safe from the weather. Consider an e-reader as a gift for the readers on your list. They can carry as many books as they like on vacation and still have room for souvenirs in their bags.

Additions

For days at the pool or sightseeing in sunny locations, you can't go wrong with trendy UV-protection sunglasses. Give them a new swimsuit, a colorful sarong, or goggles and masks for swimming and snorkeling if they're going on a summer vacation to the Caribbean or the Mediterranean. New hiking boots or water-resistant shoes are a terrific gift for people who are traveling to places with fjords, snow-capped mountains, and hiking paths.

Airline tickets

Why not make up the cost for their flights if they have a cruise booked but haven't yet bought airfare? With Flights by Celebrity, you can personalize your air route depending on your chosen airline while still earning airline points.

Is it better to use a GoPro or a camera?

Most visitors take photos with their iPhones, but being too engrossed in a device might take you out of the moment when on vacation. Instead, give them a couple of disposable cameras and urge them to document their memories on the spur of the moment.

When the film is finished, they'll remember their favorite scenes. Alternatively, give them a waterproof camera or a GoPro to document their exciting shore excursions. Whether they're snorkeling in gorgeous Caribbean waters with dolphins in the distance or marveling at European architecture and its particular, Old World beauty, they'll bring home wonderful footage of their adventures.

Packages for Special Occasions

Vacation memories will last a lifetime. Celebrity Cruises offers experience seminars, culinary cruises, and package deals for life's special occasions. Choose from three tiers of Celebration Packages to recognize their greatest achievements and happiest days for an anniversary, birthday, or wedding celebration.

A champagne breakfast delivered to their cabin, reservations for two at a specialized restaurant of your choice, and a customized cake, for example, are all included in the Premium Package. When the evening arrives, they will be presented with a rose bouquet, chocolate-dipped strawberries, and a bottle of champagne.

Gift Cards & Certificates for Cruises

With a full cruise gift certificate, you can treat your loved one to a cruise. All they have to do is pack because the cruise cost, government fees, taxes, and fuel supplement charges are all included.

Choose from a variety of gift cards ranging from $25 to $500 that they may spend toward a new reservation. There are never any fees associated with them, and they have no expiration date. They can put their gift card toward a special occasion cruise, such as a birthday party, a family reunion, or an upcoming anniversary.

Flowers to Their Suite

No matter what the occasion, receiving a flower arrangement is a memorable experience. A fresh bouquet of beautiful flowers will greet them as they enter their suite or stateroom.

Roses in passionate red, vivid yellow, or soft pink should be used to decorate their suite or stateroom. Send them a vase of hand-picked tropical flowers to brighten their day. They'll think of you as they savor a leisurely breakfast in bed or prepare for the day's seaside adventures.

Platters and Fine Wine

After you've said "goodbye," your lover or loved one is unlikely to expect any more considerate surprises from you. Sending them a bottle of champagne or an excellent cabernet to savor on their balcony is the ideal gift. From our assortment, you can select from dozens of award-winning wines and excellent spirits. Send along gastronomic treats like a gourmet tapas plate and a cheese board, or enhance the romance with a dozen chocolate-drizzled strawberries and tantalizing tiramisu if they're foodies who enjoy an elegant platter of savories and sumptuous desserts.

Souvenirs

Remember that duty-free shopping on your ship (and in many port cities) may sweeten the deal on fantastic gifts for the entire family back home before you depart on your own cruise excursion. Exclusive things such as expensive watches and high-end fragrances are available onboard. Take a stroll through the art gallery and place a bid at auction on a one-of-a-kind piece for the artists and fine art collectors in your life. Bring back spices and local rum from the Caribbean, or fresh Kona coffee beans straight from the Big Island for the foodie in your family. They'll taste exquisite Mexican chocolate, collect little trinkets from Western Europe, and love locally created Alaska mementos.

Onboard Credit

Not sure what to do with your in-laws while they're on a cruise? Perhaps you'd want to give your loved one an experience rather than a physical item? The ideal solution is to use onboard credit. Your friend or family member can book a once-in-a-lifetime dinner at a specialty restaurant with an innovative menu created by a Michelin-starred chef with the gift of an extra onboard credit.

They can go on a thrilling beach excursion that they might not have been able to go on otherwise, or they might have an additional glass of wine with dinner. Their luxurious trip will be elevated to new heights with onboard credit or the gift of an amenities package.

A Boat Trip

A bouquet of flowers or onboard credit may not seem like a large enough statement to demonstrate how much you care about the cruise enthusiast in your life. Give them a cruise as a gift. The gift of a cruise vacation will be remembered long after they have opened their ticket. You'll make it possible for the special cruiser in your life to enjoy days of leisure at sea, cultural immersion, and unforgettable memories.

Are you ready to lavish these wonderful cruise gift ideas on your loved ones? For more ideas, go to celebritycruises.com and look at cruise itineraries from all around the world.

Chapter-28

On a cruise, there are 19 things you should avoid doing

Cruising is one of the most convenient ways to travel because of the diverse sights and sounds at each new port of call, thrilling onshore excursions, and culinary delights both onboard and in port. Knowing what not to do on a cruise is just as important as knowing what to do on any other trip.

Traveling on a cruise ship is unlike any other way of viewing the world. Your accommodations will accompany you on your journey, avoiding the need to book several hotels, rush to catch the final train or look for tour operators. A cruise simplifies the decision-making process for many passengers while allowing them to relax to their full potential.

Learn what not to do on a cruise by following these guidelines.

1: Do not just pick any itinerary

Have you ever fantasized about relaxing on a white-sand beach in a tropical location? Do you want to go to far-flung regions filled with historic ruins and breathtaking natural wonders? Perhaps you're looking for a once-in-a-lifetime trip to Alaska's glaciers or Antarctica's frigid landscapes. Consider the type of trip you want before booking a cruise, and then look at itineraries that visit those locations.

You should also think about how lengthy the itinerary is. If this is your first cruise or you just have a limited amount of vacation time, a three-day cruise is a good place to start. If you have more time on your hands, a lengthier cruise might be the best option.

2: Take advantage of shore excursions

The shore excursions available at each port of call are an important component of the cruise experience. Hiking to a waterfall through tough, hilly terrain to taking a leisurely private motorcoach tour of a city's most notable attractions are examples of activities. Booking an excursion is a convenient way to immerse yourself in each location without having to worry about transportation and tours. You'll also be assured to return to the ship before it sails to the next port if you schedule an excursion.

3: Don't bring the wrong clothes

One of the most crucial things to avoid on a cruise is bringing the wrong attire. Your cruise packing list will differ depending on your destination, the time of year you sail, the weather in the area, and what you want to do while in port. Even if you're cruising to the Caribbean, carry a pair of sneakers if you plan on going on active adventures. If you plan to visit holy sites, bring something to protect your knees and shoulders. Bring something dressier to supper on Evening Chic nights. When you're outside at night or in the air conditioning, bringing a light jacket or cardigan is always a good idea.

4: Don't forget to bring your necessities

Make sure your carry-on contains everything you'll need, including sunscreen, sunglasses, medications, and water. For sunny destinations, a hat is also a good option.

5: Don't forget to bring your passport with you

(Or anywhere else for that matter.) It's a good idea to keep track of where your passport is at all times, whether at home or on vacation. Each cruise suite has a safe in which you can keep your belongings.

6: Don't overlook the importance of photographs

The ability to capture movies, images, and recollections is an important aspect of the trip experience. Bring your preferred camera as well as all the accessories you'll need to capture those unforgettable moments. Our onboard photography staff is there to assist you when you need a group shot or want to leave your trip photos in the hands of a professional.

7: Make sure you don't arrive late or lose track of time

You want to make the most of your time here. Arrive early to make the most of your time, and keep track of how long you have to finish your task. Keep in mind that other passengers rely on one another to make the cruise experience as enjoyable as possible. Furthermore, your guide is dedicated to ensuring that everyone returns to the ship securely and on time.

8: Don't be the last person to board the ship

The worst-case situation is missing your ship (which may be really embarrassing), but you also don't want to be the last one on board, so keep in mind the time zone the port is in. If the ship and the port are in separate time zones, the ship's time will often differ from the port's. If you're on a self-guided tour of a destination or traveling alone, setting a timer on your phone is a fantastic method to keep track of time.

9: Don't spend all of your time in one restaurant or pub

The spice of life is varied, and your entire dining experience will have an impact on your holiday. On this trip, foodies and finicky eaters alike will find lots of delectable selections. Onboard, there are a variety of supplementary and specialty restaurants where you may try a variety of cuisines.

Enjoy delectable sashimi, visit the raw bar, or dine on comfort foods like burgers and pizza. Why limit yourself to just one thing you enjoy?

10: Don't be frightened to venture out on your own

Booking a solo cruise or embarking on a shore excursion can be a really liberating experience. On a cruise, you'll meet thousands of new individuals, from your cabin deck neighbors to the crew, which brings us to the following point.

11: Don't be afraid to speak up!

Meeting new people is one of the most enjoyable aspects of traveling. On a cruise, you can socialize with new people over meals or beverages, join your group for games or entertainment, or go on shore excursions together. When you're all traveling to the same wonderful destinations on a luxury cruise ship, it's easy to strike up a discussion. Reminisce about your favorite trip experience to date or share your plans for the next day's schedule.

12: Do not overindulge in the breadbasket

With gratis dining, you can order a variety of appetizers or meals for your table to try. Instead of loading up on the breadbasket before dinner arrives, take advantage of the opportunity to explore things you might not order at home.

Each of the ship's dozen specialty eateries transports you to a different part of the globe. Sushi and sashimi are popular in Japan. At sea, an Italian trattoria. A Paris cafe or a French boulangerie At Luminae, dine on delicacies created by a Michelin-starred chef, or at Le Petit Chef, watch as your interactive tabletop brings food to life with the help of a little, animated chef.

13: Do not be frightened to inquire

Your cruise ship's personnel is there to assist you. They'll have an answer for you, no matter how big or small your question is. Do you want to learn more about the places you'll be visiting? Need a recommendation for a shore trip or assistance making a restaurant reservation? Use the expertise of destination concierges, shore excursion specialists, maître d's, stateroom attendants, and other crew members to make your holiday the best it can be.

14: Don't forget about your welcoming team

The personnel onboard works diligently to ensure that your cruise is everything you dreamed of and more. They are normally working behind the scenes, are always pleasant, and will comply with whatever requests you may have (within reason, of course). A simple grin and a "hello" or "good morning" to a crew member can go a long way toward demonstrating your gratitude for the hard work they put in to make your trip a success. You can always tip members of the crew if you want to go any further.

15: Don't forget to stay for the evening entertainment

The cruise industry's onboard entertainment has become something of a trademark. Many ships now have aboard state-of-the-art, full-sized theatres that will transport you to the opera in Milan or a Broadway production in New York City. Mainstage comedy acts, intimate acoustic performances, and Broadway-style shows with world-class entertainers are all part of the entertainment.

16: If you don't have to, avoid taking elevators

On cruise ships, elevators can be congested. Consider taking the stairs if you only have to go up a couple of decks.

Waiting for the elevators can take longer than walking to the next deck, yet some passengers aboard the ship rely on them for transportation.

17: Don't forget to get your money exchanged

If you're going on a cruise to several nations, be sure you know what money they use before you go. Because some smaller shops, taxi drivers, and restaurants may not accept credit cards, it's a good idea to bring some local cash with you.

18: Beverage packages should not be overlooked

Adding a beverage package to your cruise is a simple way to relax and enjoy yourself without having to worry about a surprise charge at the end of your holiday. Whether you want to enjoy specialty beers and cocktails, quality coffee in the morning, or a soda with lunch, different cruise drink packages cater to different needs. There are other packages designed specifically for children.

19: Make sure you choose the right cruise line

Decide what's most essential to you before booking a cruise with a specific cruise line. Do you want to go on a luxurious vacation? Do you have a specific level of service in mind? Are you a gourmet seeking a once-in-a-lifetime eating experience? On every cruise, you can enjoy amazing destinations, smart service, luxury accommodations, and culinary excellence. On the website, you can look up cruise itineraries and learn about all of the amazing places they visit throughout the world.

Chapter-29

Which Way Should I Wrap It Up?

While on vacation, you should expect to have a fantastic time on board a cruise ship. On the liner, there are more activities than in many resorts. You'll also have the chance to visit places you've only read about or imagined visiting. Cruises don't have to be prohibitively expensive, as this book demonstrates. They are truly within reach of the average Joe. It only takes a little ingenuity to have a fantastic time.

Even a daily budget of $20 may provide something new and exciting every day. You can buy 2-3 beers one day, gamble one night, have wine with dinner, buy a tiny photograph, obtain cheap t-shirts from ports, which make fantastic mementos for friends, especially when four for $10, or go to a different restaurant for supper. You simply cannot do everything every day!

Experienced cruisers have some closing thoughts that I believe are appropriate.

"Most crucial tip of all, forget all your troubles back home and just rest and be pampered!" they advise. In our daily lives, most of us don't have that option!" Rhonda Spruill.

"Have a good time and be prepared to do something you wouldn't normally do!" Bradley J. Edmonds, Ph.D.

"Like everything else in life, you get out of a cruise what you put into it."
-Wanda Foster is a writer.

Above all, don't believe the phrase "once in a lifetime opportunity!"

That mindset could be the reason why some individuals lose their brains and become irrational. You'll be better able to stick to your budget if you keep it in mind. Take lots of movies and absorb in the moments you've had while saving money for your future cruise adventure instead of accumulating additional goods that will end up in a garage sale.

References
www.cruisemates.com
www.cruisediva.com
www.cruisecritic.com

Made in the USA
Coppell, TX
23 July 2022